D0368515

CHRIST

AND THE

BELIEVER

IN

THE SONG OF SONGS

CHRIST

AND THE

BELIEVER

IN

THE SONG OF SONGS

by

WENDELL P. LOVELESS

Director, WMBI, WDLM
Member of faculty, Moody Bible Institute
Author of *Sunrise Meditations, Little Talks on Great Words*
Compiler of *Radio Songs and Choruses*

MOODY PRESS

153 Institute Place Chicago, Illinois

Printed in the United States of America

This book is affectionately dedicated

to

WILLIAM L. PETTINGILL, D.D.,

through whom I received, early in my Christian experience, an example of the fruitfulness of simple, practical, Bible exposition, as well as that of a genuine, joyous Christian life.

PREFACE

IN PRESENTING these Devotional Studies in the Song of Solomon, I feel that a few explanatory remarks may be in order.

For several years it has been in my heart to prepare a series of studies in this rich portion of the Old Testament, which would be sufficiently simple to meet the needs of "babes in Christ"; sufficiently satisfying to feed the hearts of more mature believers; and, at the same time, presented in such a form that Sunday school teachers, leaders of Young People's and Bible Study groups might use them as a foundation in passing along the truth to others. It is my sincere hope that this book may, in some measure at least, meet those needs.

The method of approach to the Song of Songs, as found in this book, may be quite new to many of our readers, but it is my prayer that through the study, the sweetness and fragrance of the Person of Christ may be recognized and appropriated to the great blessing of those who read.

These studies are not intended to be exhaustive, for there is much of analysis and exegesis which has not been attempted. There is much rich ore in the way of typical study which has not been mined at all. And the wide and interesting phase of the type as it concerns Jehovah and Israel, His "wife," has only been touched upon. The main objective, as the title of the book implies, is to emphasize the eternal, indissoluble, and unspeakably precious relationship between Christ, the Heavenly Bridegroom, and each individual believer, as well as the Church "which is His Body."

May the Holy Spirit be pleased to use these pages in such a way that our Lord Jesus Christ shall be exalted in our lives, to the end that truly we may "know Him, and make Him known."

WENDELL P. LOVELESS

FOREWORD

OF ALL the neglected portions of the Word of God, it seems as though the Song of Solomon is most ignored. Indeed, many Christians share the aversion of some early Church Fathers, who doubted the canonicity of the book. Without any thought of limiting our gaze to one volume in the divine library, but with praiseworthy purpose to bring to our view that which otherwise might have escaped us, the author of this study serves us.

The material on these pages, in abbreviated fashion, was given in connection with the Radio School of the Bible, a regular feature of the radio stations of the Moody Bible Institute. The author's plan of development—different, simple, helpful—will suggest one of the reasons he has such large enrollments in the radio school—no mean feat, when the pupils cannot see the teacher!

This book is not a commentary on the Canticles; it is more. Of course, there is interpretation of the sacred text, but there is as well heart-warming, stimulating, practical comment. Blest indeed will he be, who, united with the Lord by faith, learns the joy of communion as set forth by the author. May the Lord's blessing rest upon this book and upon those who receive instruction from its pages.

William Culbertson, D.D.
Dean, Moody Bible Institute

CHARACTERS IN THE SONG OF SOLOMON, IN THE ORDER IN WHICH THEY SPEAK

The Bride	Chapter	1, verses	2 to 7
The Bridegroom	"	1, "	8 to 11
The Bride	"	1, "	12 to 14
The Bridegroom	"	1, "	15
The Bride	"	1, "	16 and 17
	"	2, "	1
The Bridegroom	"	2, "	2
The Bride	"	2, "	3 to 6
The Bridegroom	"	2, "	7
The Bride	"	2, "	8 to "me" in verse 10
The Bridegroom	"	2, "	10 ("Rise") to 15
The Bride	"	2, "	16 and 17
	"	3, "	1 to 4
The Bridegroom	"	3, "	5
The Bride	"	3, "	6 to 11
The Bridegroom	"	4, "	1 to 5
The Bride	"	4, "	6
The Bridegroom	"	4, "	7 to "out" in verse 16
The Bride	"	4, "	16 from "Let"
The Bridegroom	"	5, "	1
The Bride	"	5, "	2 to 8
Daughters of Jerusalem	"	5, "	9

The Bride	Chapter 5, verses 10 to 16
Daughters of Jerusalem	" 6, " 1
The Bride	" 6, " 2 and 3
The Bridegroom	" 6, " 4 to 9
Daughters of Jerusalem	" 6, " 10
The Bridegroom	" 6, " 11 and 12
Daughters of Jerusalem	" 6, " 13
The Bridegroom	" 7, " 1 to 9
The Bride	" 7, " 10 to 13
	" 8, " 1 to 3
The Bridegroom	" 8, " 4
Daughters of Jerusalem	" 8, " 5 to "beloved"
The Bridegroom	" 8, " 5 from "I"
The Bride	" 8, " 6 to 8
The Bridegroom	" 8, " 9
The Bride	" 8, " 10 to 12
The Bridegroom	" 8, " 13
The Bride	" 8, " 14

SONG OF SOLOMON

Introductory

In I Corinthians 2:14, we are told that "the natural man receiveth not the things of the Spirit of God: for they are foolishness unto him: neither can he know them, because they are spiritually discerned."

Of no Bible book is this more true than of the Song of Solomon.

To some it is veiled in deep mystery.

To some—perhaps overly ascetic, it may seem in poor taste.

To others, it appears to be a bit of Oriental romantic verse, nothing more.

But some, who have been born again, and who have tasted of the preciousness of the Person of the Lord Jesus, will see in this a love song of exquisite beauty.

Has it not been true always that a message of love has been a special, personal message to the one who personally receives it? It is fully understood by no other.

So with the love of God in Christ. He loves *all,* but He loves *each,* and the expressions of His love are intensely individual and personal.

There must be the responsive heart, if one is to hear and appreciate the words and music of His song of love.

Solomon, the writer of this song, was a gifted composer. In I Kings 4:32 we are told that he composed a thousand and five songs. Evidently this song is the choice one of his compositions, for he calls it "The Song of Songs," or more literally, "The Song which excels all other songs."

Solomon wrote the book of Ecclesiastes in the last years of his life; he wrote the book of Proverbs during the years of middle age; and evidently the Song of Songs was composed during the years of his youth—the years of ardent love. In this love song we detect the various, subtle emotions attendant upon impassioned wooing—sometimes thwarted, sometimes sweetly successful.

In an appreciative study of the Song, we must view it *historically,* as being a partial record of Solomon's actual marital experiences; *typically,* as being an illustration of Jehovah's relations as Husband to Israel, His wife, and the relationship between Christ and His bride, the true Church; *practically,* as containing precious exhortations, warnings and consolations for the individual believer of this age of grace.

There is a very profitable typical study in a consideration of the Song as it applies to God's Covenant people Israel—in communion with Jehovah, then with communion broken through sin and disobedience, and finally restored to the place of blessing and fruitfulness. The Old Testament prophetical books contain this sad and yet glorious narrative.

But we shall be occupied chiefly with the typical picture as it relates to the indissoluble relationship between the Lord Jesus and the Christian.

As we approach a devotional and practical meditation upon this portion of Holy Scripture, it is well to remind ourselves that there is a difference between *union* and *communion.*

There may be *junction* without *unction.*

One observes some marriages where there is *union,* but apparently very little, if any, *communion.*

We fear that this difference is all too apparent in the case of some true children of God. When they received Christ as Saviour and were born again by grace through faith, there was instant and eternal union—they were joined to Christ in a welded union which can never be dissolved during time or eternity.

And yet, while this is gloriously true as to positional relationship, there may be little real heart communion, little genuine appreciation of the lovely Person of our Lord, little time spent in personal and loving fellowship.

It is wondrously true that the believer's *union* with Christ can never be annulled. There is eternal guarantee in God's Word for that.

But it is also sadly true that *communion* may be broken.

And when it is broken there is an interruption of joy, peace, fellowship and fruitfulness in service.

The design of this Song of Songs is to set forth the wondrous fact of *union,* and the resultant blessings of *communion.*

The key to it all is a Person—the altogether lovely Lord Jesus, the heavenly Bridegroom who loves His own with an everlasting love, and woos His loved one with a persistence and patience so characteristic of Himself.

We shall think of this study along lines which are a bit unusual. Instead of a verse-by-verse exposition, we shall consider rather groups of verses under six general heads:

I. What the Bride says about the Bridegroom
II. What the Bridegroom says about the Bride
III. What the Bride says about herself
IV. What the Bridegroom says about Himself
V. What the Daughters of Jerusalem say about the Bride
VI. What the Daughters of Jerusalem say about the Bridegroom.

And then, under each general heading, we shall meditate upon four thoughts:

1. The *Declaration*
2. The Typical *Implication*
3. The New Testament *Revelation*
4. The Practical *Application.*

Thus we shall hope to find some truths made precious to our hearts in a manner which shall bring forth much fruit in our lives.

While the emphasis in our study is to be upon the spiritual and devotional aspects, we must not overlook the message which the Song of Solomon has along the line of the sacredness and beauty of true married love.

In a day when some, in the name of advanced piety and "purity of life," would place restrictions and impose prohibitions upon the marriage relationship, one needs to read this Song with but casual discernment to observe that it is "the vindication of marital love against both asceticism and lust."

Let not man, however high the motive, interfere with God-given prerogatives in divinely established human relationships.

It is a divinely established principle that to *know* Christ, one must *love* Him. So saith the Apostle in I Corinthians 8:3, ". . . if any man love God, the same is known of him." As another has pointed out, "This is why the Song of Solomon offers such a wonderful contrast to the Book of Ecclesiastes, which immediately precedes it. There the object pursued is *knowledge,* and the end is *vanity;* here the object pursued is *love,* and the end is *satisfaction.* You can never know God by searching, but love to God is the gate to the knowledge of God. And the first step toward love to God is believing God's love to us. 'We love him, because he first loved us'" (I John 4:19).

Section One

SONG OF SOLOMON 1:1-2:7

LET us reverently and thoughtfully enter upon a consideration of our first division.

I. WHAT THE BRIDE SAYS ABOUT THE BRIDEGROOM

1. *THE DECLARATION*

A. 1:2—". . . thy love is better than wine."

B. 1:3—". . . thy name is as ointment poured forth."

C. 1:4—"Draw me, we will run after thee."

D. 1:4—". . . the king hath brought me into his chambers."

E. 1:4—". . . we will be glad and rejoice in thee."

F. 1:7—"Tell me . . . where thou feedest, where thou madest thy flock to rest at noon."

G. 1:13—"A bundle of myrrh is my well-beloved unto me."

H. 1:14—"My beloved is unto me as a cluster of camphire (cypress) in the vineyards of En-gedi."

I. 1:16—"Behold, thou art fair, my beloved, yea, pleasant."

J. 2:3—"As the apple tree among the trees of the wood, so is my beloved among the sons."

K. 2:3—". . . his fruit was sweet to my taste."

L. 2:4—"He brought me to the banqueting house, and his banner over me was love."

2. *THE TYPICAL IMPLICATION*

In this entire section, while the Bride is speaking to and of the object of her heart's affection, the Bridegroom, we hear precious echoes, typically, of the cry of the believer's heart, who is truly in love with the Lord Jesus.

As we proceed with our study, we shall discover that every phase—and more—of the pure marital relationship, typified the unspeakably blessed relationship between the Lord Jesus and the objects of His love.

Some readers and students of the Bible are inclined either to overlook or deliberately ignore the types of the Old Testament. Those who overlook them have, for the most part, been deprived of the kind of Bible exposition which unfolds the beauties of them. Those who ignore them are usually fearful lest they prove to be fantastic and fabulous. Unquestionably some, in presenting typical teaching, have gone beyond legitimate bounds, and thus have brought disrepute upon this entire school of thought. But to those who, guided by the Holy Spirit, take a sane scriptural path in such study, God's Old Testament "Picture Book" yields "acres of diamonds" and "nuggets of gold" which are not discovered in any other way.

The typical emphasis, in this section, as it relates to the Bride's thoughts toward the Bridegroom, is upon the nature of ideal communion. And the ground of such communion is threefold—first, the Person of Christ; second, a yielded believer; and lastly, Christ put first in every department of the believer's thought and life.

3. *THE NEW TESTAMENT REVELATION*

In the following New Testament references, the capital letters refer back to those under roman numeral I, "The *DECLARATION*," and are the New Testament counterpart of the Bride's utterances.

A. Ephesians 3:19—". . . to know the *love* of Christ, which passeth (mere human) knowledge." Also I John 4:18.

B. Philippians 2:9, 10—"Wherefore God also hath highly exalted him, and given him a *name* which is above every name: That at the *name* of Jesus every knee should bow."

C. Hebrews 12:1, 2—". . . let us lay aside every weight, and the sin which doth so easily beset us, and let us *run* with patience the race that is set before us, looking unto Jesus . . ."

D. Colossians 2:2—". . . being knit together in love."

E. Philippians 4:4—*"Rejoice* in the Lord alway: and again I say, *Rejoice."*

F. Matthew 11:28—"Come unto me, all ye that labour and are heavy laden, and I will give you rest."

G. II Corinthians 2:14—"Now thanks be unto God, which always causeth us to triumph (leadeth us in triumph, R.V.) in Christ, and maketh manifest the *savour* of his knowledge by us in every place."

H. II Corinthians 2:15—"For we are unto God a *sweet savour* of Christ . . ."

I. Colossians 2:9—"For in him (Christ) dwelleth all the fulness of the Godhead bodily."

J. Colossians 2:7—"Rooted and built up in him . . ." Also Revelation 22:2—John 6:56-58.

K. Galatians 5:22, 23—"But the fruit of the Spirit (Christ) is love, joy, peace, longsuffering, gentleness, goodness, faith (faithfulness), meekness, temperance: against such there is no law."

L. John 6:35—"And Jesus said unto them, I am the bread of life: he that cometh to me shall never hunger; and he that believeth on me shall never thirst."

4. *THE PRACTICAL APPLICATION*

Again, in this portion of our study, as in that under the figure "3," the capital letters refer to the scripture references under roman numeral I.

A. 1:2—". . . thy love is better than wine."

In a most excellent commentary upon the Song of Songs by Annie W. Marston, the writer points out several ways in which the love of Christ is "better than wine."

a. *WINE* "maketh glad the heart" (Psalm 104:15). But "at the last it biteth like a serpent and stingeth like an adder" (Prov. 23:32). Not so with *His love.* It is the same yesterday, and today, and forever. He loveth "unto the end" (John 13:1).

b. *WINE* "causeth the lips of those that are asleep to speak" (Song of Solomon 7:9). But *His love* raiseth the *dead* (Luke 7:15).

c. *WINE* "makes our eyes to behold strange things" (Prov. 23:33 R.V.). *His love* causes us to see, not unreal phantoms of a muddled brain, but "the wonders of His dying love and our own worthlessness."

d. *WINE* was given "that such as be faint in the wilderness may drink" (II Sam. 16:2). But it was only a little later, in II Samuel 17:29, that these same were again "weary and thirsty in the wilderness." *His love* gives power to the faint that they may "walk, and not faint" (Isa. 40:31).

e. *WINE* is given to "those that be of heavy hearts" (Prov. 31:6), only to give *temporary* relief from their misery and woe. *His love* guarantees that we shall have *permanent* forgetfulness of the misery from which He has saved us (Isaiah 54:4; Hebrews 10:17).

f. *WINE* overcomes a man and leaves him weak and trembling, and makes him reel and stagger (Psalm 107:27). *His love* overcomes us, and makes us "more than conquerors through Him that loved us" (Romans 8:37). Oh, blessed Lord, thy love is better than wine!

B. 1:3—". . . thy name is as ointment poured forth."

To the heart of the believer, enjoying true communion with his Lord, the name of the Lord Jesus is most fragrant. His *name* is Himself. It is the expression of all that He *is:* His loveliness, His grace, His excellency, His purity, His power, His perfection.

But it is as ointment *poured forth.* The Bride does not enjoy it to the exclusion of others. Those associated with her share in its sweetness.

What a lesson for us here. We are *channels,* not *reservoirs.* The beauty and fragrance of Christ will flow through us if the channel is clear.

And, as one has expressed it, "the more of Christ we share with others, the more we have of Christ to share." What a fellowship, and what a glorious privilege!

C. 1:4—"Draw me, we will run after thee."

Did you notice the change from the singular to the plural form of the pronoun?

"Draw *me; we* will run after thee."

The one who truly has been attracted by the Person of Christ, longs to run after Him, to follow Him.

That one soon learns that even our desire for Him, and ability to "run after" Him are only the result of His *drawing*.

And we soon learn also that when the individual believer is *drawn*, and responds in *running*—ready, quick obedience—*others* will be drawn also.

"Draw *me, we* will run." That is the inevitable result. It is God's way. It is the reproductive scheme of obedient fellowship.

It is important to note that it is running *after Him*. Not after other Christians, no matter how able and consecrated, but *"after Thee."*

A young missionary once said, "I shall never be able to go too fast, while the Lord is in front of me (John 10:4), and I never can go too slowly, if I follow Him always, everywhere."

The true test of fruitful service is seen in the record of John the Baptist, in John 1:37, "and the two disciples heard him (John) speak, and they followed *Jesus*." Not John, but Jesus. That is it—John was drawn, and those who heard him ran after Jesus.

We may "run" with confidence and assurance (Heb. 12:1), because the One who draws "goeth before" (John 10:4).

But we do not run as those in a panic and beset with fear, but, as the contestant in the game, who is looking forward to the prize at the end of the race.

D. 1:4—". . . the king hath brought me into his chambers."

See how quickly her prayer was answered. She asks him that he draw her, and pledges that she and her companions will run after him, but he does "exceeding abundantly above all that she asks," and she testifies "he *hath brought* me into his chambers."

Our Lord would bring each one of His own into this inner sanctuary "To behold the beauty of the Lord, and to enquire in his temple" (Psalm 27:4).

He wants us to come to know and appreciate Himself. And so He *brings* us. Sometimes it is through sorrow, and affliction, and chastening, but He *brings* us. The power to bring us is His own. He uses His own methods. But the hands which *bring* us are tender, nail-pierced hands!

E. 1:4—". . . we will be glad and rejoice *in thee*."

He is the secret and source of all true gladness and joy. The Psalmist sang, "Thou hast put gladness in my heart" (Psalm 4:7), and Nehemiah 8:10 declares, ". . . the joy of the Lord is your strength."

There is a vast difference between *happiness* and *joy*. Happiness depends upon *happenings,* and when the happenings are pleasant, all is well; but when otherwise, happiness flies out the window. Not so with true *gladness* and *joy* which are gifts of the Lord to His people.

They are not destroyed by circumstances, by sorrow, by disappointments, by changes in plans, by afflictions or trials. True joy transcends all these.

The Bride assures the Bridegroom that joy will be found "in *thee*." She will not look for joy in her feelings, or her pleasant circumstances, or her fellowship with others, or her spiritual state, or her "religious exercises," but in Himself.

"Satisfied with Thee, Lord Jesus,
I am blest,
Peace which passeth understanding
On Thy breast;
No more doubting, no more trembling,
O, what rest!"

F. 1:7—"Tell me . . . where thou feedest, where thou makest thy flock to rest at noon."

The true believer has discovered that there is no genuine rest and refreshment apart from Christ, and longs after the rest which He alone can give. He has said, "Come unto me . . . and I will give you rest" (Matt. 11:28).

There is a beautiful touch in this plea of the Bride. She acknowledges that the Shepherd *makest* His flock to rest. How great is the faithfulness of our Lord! One is reminded of the words in Psalm 23:2, "He *maketh* me to lie down in green pastures."

Our Lord has many ways of *making* us reach the place of true "rest." There is the "rest of *faith*" for *salvation.* There is the rest of *assurance* as we fully believe His written Word. There is the rest of *service* when we realize that the work is the Lord's and we are but instruments in His hands, for the accomplishment of His purposes.

Sometimes He employs sorrow to "make us lie down," sometimes affliction, sometimes the affectionate glance of wounded love, as in the case of Simon Peter after he had denied the Lord. But to the yielded believer, all of these paths lead to "green pastures" and "the rest at noon," in the heat and confusion of the day.

No matter how far we wander from the path, we are not too far for His love, His power, His "rod and staff."

And it is worthy of note that this same one who, in verse 4, had been eager to "run after" the Bridegroom, is now eager to enjoy the rest of fellowship. There is a time to *run,* and a time to *rest.* Both are important. But the Lord Jesus' interview with Martha and Mary in the home in Bethany left no doubt as to the "better part." The most fruitful Christ-life and service is the one which has learned the holy secret of doing the *running* with *restfulness* of heart and spirit. That secret prevents "nervous breakdowns" among the Lord's ministers, and service performed in the "energy of the flesh."

G. 1:13—"A bundle of myrrh is my well beloved unto me."

H. 1:14—"My beloved is unto me as a cluster of camphire (cypress) in the vineyards of En-gedi."

In Oriental lands a bundle of myrrh hidden in the bosom gave fragrance to the garments and to all around, at home or abroad. This source of sweetness was hidden from the eye in the breast.

But the cluster of camphire, or cypress, was carried openly in the hand. It was beautiful to *see,* as well as fragrant.

The bundle of myrrh and the cluster of camphire speak of the two-fold thought expressed by the Apostle, "That Christ may dwell *in your hearts* by faith" (Eph. 3:17), and "Always bearing about in the body the dying of the Lord Jesus, that the life also of Jesus might be made manifest in our body" (II Cor. 4:10).

We are told that the vineyards of En-gedi were famous for their fruits and spices. All that was beautiful to look upon, pleasant to the taste, and fragrant, was found there in profusion. Such is our altogether lovely Lord to us. And it is our privilege, yea, our high responsibility to so represent Him in the world that Christ crucified, risen, exalted, and glorified shall be seen in and through us. There must be the myrrh in the bosom, Christ in the heart, but the cluster of camphire, Christ in the *life,* also must be seen.

I. 1:16—"Behold, thou art fair, my beloved, yea, pleasant."

The Bridegroom, in verse 15, had used words very similar to these in addressing the bride. He had twice called her "fair."

But here, in verse 16, when the Bride responds you will note that she doesn't speak of herself at all, but her thoughts are all of Him.

There is an important lesson here. When the Bridegroom speaks in such glowing terms of His Bride, she does not even speak of her unworthiness. She does not say that she is unworthy of His love. This is true humility. True humility is not in speaking ill of one's self, but in not thinking of one's self at all.

So many times we are apt to be occupied with our unworthiness and our badness, and at the same time have proud hearts. Pride is most subtle, and, if we are not watchful, we shall feel ourselves to be so humble that we shall be proud of it.

Grace has lifted us into the heavenlies in Christ. We are "accepted in Him," "complete in Him," "dead with Him," "risen with Him," "seated with Him in the heavenlies" (Eph. 1; Col. 2). He desires that our response to all of this marvelous working shall be a heart taken up completely with Himself, and others—not ourselves.

He asks us to "humble ourselves" (I Pet. 5:6), but He does not want us to be occupied with our humility. The Apostle, in Ephesians 5:18, exhorts us to "be filled with the (Holy) Spirit," but we are not to be occupied with our fulness. The true objective is that our occupation shall be with Him.

"The bird that soars on highest wing,
Builds on the ground her lowly nest;
And she that doth most sweetly sing,
Sings in the shade when all things rest.
In lark and nightingale we see
What honor hath humility.

"When Mary chose the better part,
She meekly sat at Jesus' feet.
And Lydia's gently opened heart
Was made for God's own temple meet.
Fairest and best adorned is she
Whose clothing is humility.

"The saint that wears heaven's brightest crown
In humble adoration bends;
The weight of glory bows him down,
Then most, when most, his soul ascends
Nearest the throne must ever be,
The footstool of humility."

It is precious to note, in verse 16, the plural form of the pronoun "our," when the bride says *"our* bed is green." It is like the words "us," "we," "with" in Ephesians. It suggests indissoluble union of Christ and the believer. It is *welded* union! Eternal union! Absolute, complete, and everlasting identification with Christ. We are one with Christ, and one with one another. We are one in life, one in acceptance, one in glory! He said (John 14:20), "ye in me, and I in you." Seven words of one syllable each, but they tell a story which it will take eternity to fully unfold.

J. 2:3—"As the apple tree among the trees of the wood, so is my beloved among the sons."
K. 2:3—". . . his fruit was sweet to my taste."

Those who are familiar with the trees of Oriental lands, tell us that the apple tree, so familiar to us in this country, is not the tree mentioned in verse 3, but rather the citron-tree which grows in Palestine. It has thick foliage to furnish abundant shade, and its fruit is lovely to taste.

The form of expression in verse 3 is significant, "among the trees of the wood." Thus the tree to which the Bride likens her Beloved is singled out as distinctive, and apart from the common, ordinary trees. It is said that the difference between this citron-tree and other trees is most striking, and when the weary, footsore traveller sees it, he rejoices to find such beauty and refreshment. So with the believer and Christ. The fruit which the world offers, "The works of the flesh" (Gal. 5:19-21), can no longer satisfy the one who has tasted of Christ. The Bride once occupied another place, the place of sin and death (Eph. 2:1), but now she is in the place which He has provided through His own finished work, and she finds Him sweet to her taste.

You will notice the order suggested in verse 3, "I sat down" . . . "his fruit was sweet." She finds *rest* first, then enjoyment of His Person. This is an infallible principle in spiritual matters. First *rest,* then enjoyment and fruitfulness.

We must be attracted to the Lord Jesus because of *what He is,* not merely for what He does. Even in Eden's garden, Eve was attracted to the tree because of that which she wanted from it. The result was spiritual, moral, and physical disaster. We "sit down under His shadow" and find Him to be all that we need.

> L. 2:4—"He brought me to the banqueting house, and his banner over me was love."

In verse 4 of chapter 1, the Bride declares that the Bridegroom had brought her into His "chambers." That is private, intimate fellowship. But here is the more public character of the relationship, into the "banqueting house," or "house of wine." Wine speaks of joy, and the *"house* of wine" suggests that it is our Lord's purpose that we shall *show forth* His praise in joyous testimony before others. The practical value of the intimacy of "the chambers" (1:4), is that it shall result in letting our light so shine before men, that they may see our good works and glorify our Father (Matt. 5:16).

The Psalmist, in Psalm 60:4, refers to the banner, "Thou hast given a banner to them that fear thee, *that it may be displayed* because of the truth."

A banner is a symbol of allegiance, of possession. "God commendeth his love toward us, in that, while we were yet sinners, Christ died for us" (Rom. 5:8). God has "so loved . . . that he *gave* his only begotten Son" (John 3:16). That love did not cease when He brought us out of death into life, through regeneration, but it continues through every moment of every day ". . . having loved his own which were in the world, he loved them unto the end" (John 13:1).

"O Love that wilt not let me go
I rest my weary soul in Thee;
I give Thee back the life I owe,
That in Thine ocean depths its flow
May richer, fuller be."

And now we come to the second main point in SECTION ONE and discover—

II. WHAT THE BRIDEGROOM SAYS ABOUT THE BRIDE

1. *THE DECLARATION*

A. 1:8—". . . O thou fairest among women."

B. 1:9—"I have compared thee, O my love, to a company of horses in Pharaoh's chariots."

C. 1:10—"Thy cheeks are comely with rows of jewels."

D. 1:10—". . . thy neck (is comely) with chains of gold."

E. 1:15—". . . thou art fair, my love; behold thou art fair."

F. 1:15—". . . thou hast dove's eyes."

G. 2:2—"As the lily among the thorns, so is my love among the daughters."

H. 2:7—"I charge you, O ye daughters of Jerusalem . . . that ye stir not up, nor awake my love, till he (she) please."

2. *THE TYPICAL IMPLICATION*

In the expressions of endearment on the part of the Bridegroom toward His bride, we hear, typically, the expressions from the heart of the Lord Jesus toward His own people.

The wonder of the grace of God in its operation is that it can reach down to poor, helpless men and women, dead in trespasses and sins, children of Adam, wholly depraved, enemies of God, alienated from God by wicked works, without any thought of God, and, so move upon those hearts and minds, until there is a conviction of sin and of utter need; then, through the process of regeneration—the new birth (John 3), by the Holy Spirit and the written Word of God, bring those same poor sinners out of death into life; out of darkness into light, partakers of the divine nature, "to an inheritance incorruptible, and undefiled, and that fadeth not away" (I Pet. 1:4). And not this merely, but "he (God) hath made him (Jesus) to be sin for us, who knew no sin; that we might *be made the righteousness of God* in him" (II Cor. 5:21).

But more, wonder of wonders, we who have believed are so completely identified with Christ, that He never sees us apart from Himself. He looks upon us "in Christ," clothed with Him who *is* the Righteousness of God.

When Balaam would curse Israel for hire (Num. 22), he was obliged to say (Num. 23:21), "He (God) hath not beheld iniquity in Jacob, neither hath he seen perverseness in Israel." Iniquity and perverseness were there, that is certain, but God, because the people of Israel was a people set apart unto Himself, accepted upon the ground of the shed blood of sacrifices, all of which pointed forward to Calvary, was able to say, "I have neither beheld nor seen iniquity or perverseness." If this were true of Jehovah and Israel, how much more can it be said concerning the relationship between Christ and the members of His body. We now may sing—

"Near, so very near to God,
Nearer I could not be;
For in the Person of His Son
I'm just as near as He.

"Dear, so very dear to God,
Dearer I could not be;
For in the Person of His Son
I'm just as dear as He."

3. *THE NEW TESTAMENT REVELATION*

A. Ephesians 1:4—"According as he hath chosen us in him before the foundation of the world, that we should be holy and without blame before him in love."

B. I Corinthians 6:20—"For ye are bought with a price: therefore glorify God in your body."

C. Ephesians 5:26, 27—"That he might sanctify and

D. cleanse it with the washing of water by the Word,

E. that he might present it to himself a glorious

F. church, not having spot, or wrinkle, or any such thing; but that it should be holy and without blemish."

G. II Corinthians 6:14—"Be ye not unequally yoked together with unbelievers: for what fellowship hath righteousness with unrighteousness? And what communion hath light with darkness?"

H. Ephesians 5:14—"Wherefore he saith, Awake thou that sleepest, and arise from the dead, and Christ shall give thee light."

4. *THE PRACTICAL APPLICATION*

A. 1:8—". . . O thou fairest among women."
E. 1:15—". . . thou art fair, my love; behold thou art fair."

When Christ is regarded as thus addressing the believer, we must not fail to realize that we are what we are by the grace of God.

We are fair because we have been declared righteous upon the ground of the shed blood of Christ (Rom. 3:25, 26).

We are fair because we are clothed with garments of beauty from the wardrobe of His grace and glory.

We are fair because we have been sanctified through the Holy Spirit (I Pet. 1:2).

We are fair because ". . . God, who commanded the light to shine out of darkness, hath shined in our hearts, to give the light of the knowledge of the glory of God in the face of Jesus Christ (II Cor. 4:6).

We are fair because we are "in Christ," and only because of that.

B. 1:9—"I have compared thee, O my love, to a company of horses in Pharaoh's chariots."

It is thought that Solomon is here making reference, not to the horses still in the stables of Egypt, but of those which Solomon purchased from Pharaoh for his own personal use. In I Kings 10:28, 29, it is recorded that ". . . Solomon had horses brought out of Egypt . . . And a chariot came up and went out of Egypt for six hundred shekels of silver, and an horse for an hundred and fifty."

The figure which the Bridegroom uses here of the Bride is a very full and significant one:

The horses were *bought* (I Cor. 6:20),
They were brought out of Egypt (the world),
They were the joy of the owner,

They were well provided for and fed,
They were swift (obedient),
They were full of life (testimony),
They were subject to the owner's will,
They were obedient to the Master's voice,
They were ready to *go,* or ready to stand still,
They were symbols of strength (Eph. 6:10),
They were called to royal service (I Pet. 2:9),
The yoke upon them was furnished by the Master (Matt. 11:30).

There was a "company" of them. We are saved to win others. The story is told of the wife who, with her two children, was crossing the ocean, when a storm wrecked the vessel and sank it. The wife was one of a very few passengers who was rescued. Upon her arrival at a port, she cabled one word to her husband. The word was "Saved." The next day she cabled a second message, "Saved *alone."*

Our God has left us in the world that we might gain "a company" for the Lord Jesus. What a privilege, and what a responsibility!

C. 1:10—"Thy cheeks are comely with rows of jewels."

D. 1:10—". . . thy neck (is comely) with chains of gold."

Here again is a remarkable suggestion that the Bridegroom finds, in the adornment of the Bride, so much to His delight.

Can it be that Christ sees in us those qualities which gladden His heart? Yes—unspeakable grace—that is true. But it must never be forgotten that these qualities in us in which He delights, are the very qualities which He has bestowed upon us in grace! Just as the bride was adorned with *gifts* received from her Beloved, so that which renders us attractive to our Lord are the gifts and bestowels of His grace. He clothes us with His own attractions, and then delights in us. What a practical incentive to holy living this should be. As the hymn so well expresses it—

> "Naught have I gotten but what I received,
> Grace hath bestowed it since I have believed;
> Boasting excluded, pride I abase;
> I'm only a sinner saved by grace!"

Jewels speak of beauty; *gold* of deity and royalty. What a calling is ours!

F. 1:15—". . . thou hast doves' eyes."

The dove, in Scripture, is a most interesting and instructive study. In the eighth chapter of Genesis we see it in connection with the Ark of God (salvation), and the olive branch (peace). When there was judgment upon the whole earth, the little dove had salvation and peace.

And we note also that the dove was offered as a sacrifice in the Levitical offerings, and thus is a type of the Lord Jesus Himself. In chapter 5, verse 12, of the Song, the Bride uses this same expression of the Bridegroom, "His eyes are as the eyes of doves." The same figure is used for Christ and the believer. Perfect union! We are called to lives of sacrifice (Rom. 12:1, 2), not to give our bodies to death, but to be "living sacrifices."

The dove is also a type of the Holy Spirit. The Holy Spirit took the form of a dove when He descended upon the Lord Jesus at the time He was baptized.

The dove mourns when it is absent from its mate.

That Christian has "dove's eyes" whose eyes are "single," and constantly "looking unto Jesus" (Heb. 12:2).

G. 2:2—"As the lily among the thorns, so is my love among the daughters."

There is a distinct contrast between lilies and thorns. The lily is a symbol of purity, while a thorn represents sin.

The Bridegroom continues His adoration of the Bride, who is to Him all that is lovely and beautiful. And here He not only likens her to the lily, but as if He would make her beauty more striking, adds, "among the thorns." She was by no means one of the thorns, but distinct and apart from them, although among them.

We are reminded of the word in John 15:19, when our Lord said to His disciples, "If ye were of the world, the world would love his own: but because ye are not of the world, but I have chosen you out of the world, therefore the world hateth you."

And again, in II Corinthians 6:17, the words of Paul, ". . . come out from among them, and be ye separate, saith the Lord, and touch not the unclean thing."

We are *in* the world, but not of the world. We are *among* thorns, but assuredly not one *of* them. The world crowned the Son of God with *thorns* (Matt. 27:29). The thorns are reserved for burning (Isa. 33:12). May we never be mistaken for a thorn by the world or by fellow believers, but rather may our Lord always find His delight in us as a "lily *among* the thorns."

A word of warning here. While we are called to paths of separation from the world and its ways, we are not called to attitudes of spiritual pride. God hates pride in the Christian as well as in others, perhaps more.

If we assume an attitude of superiority toward "the thorns" we shall soon lose our "lily" character. And, too, we can never win others to Christ if we forget that we are what we are by the grace of God.

Let us be careful *how* we separate ourselves. We are not to be Pharisees in this regard, but humble, obedient children of God, determined to walk in paths pleasing to Him.

H. 2:7—"I charge you, O ye daughters of Jerusalem, by the roes, and by the hinds of the field, that ye stir not up, nor awake my love, till he (she) please."

The original Hebrew of this passage renders the pronoun in the last clause "she" instead of "he," which is consistent with the fact that the Bridegroom is speaking.

True love cannot be forced. True love is more then mere sentimentality. To attempt to "awaken" it before all the factors are present may result in an abortive and transient counterfeit. Likewise to stir up mere emotionalism in the believer may find him "taking stands" and "forward steps" in his own strength and in the energy of the flesh.

Does not this account for much of that which passes for "conversion" in some evangelistic campaigns, and for "consecration" in meetings designed to attract believers to a closer walk with the Lord?

How vital it is to realize that the only kind of love acceptable to our Heavenly Bridegroom is "the love of God . . . shed abroad in our hearts by the Holy Spirit which is *given* unto us" (Rom. 5:5). As we are occupied with Christ, the Holy Spirit who has *given* to us the love of God, "stirs it up" within us, and *loves through us,* Godward and manward.

"The daughters of Jerusalem" to whom the Bridegroom addresses this exhortation, may well represent professing Christendom, not true believers only, but those who *profess* allegiance, although never actually entering into the blessed relationship between the Bride and Bridegroom.

And there is a most practical suggestion in the reference to the "roes" and the "hinds" in verse 7. It is said that these two animals are the most timid and easily startled in the field. They have such a keen sense of hearing that they are able to detect danger even when it is at a great distance from them. So should we be delicately sensitive to that which would, in any way, jeopardize our communion and fellowship with the Lord Jesus Christ.

We come to our third main point in SECTION ONE—

III. WHAT THE BRIDE SAYS ABOUT HERSELF

1. *THE DECLARATION*

A. 1:5—"I am black but comely . . . as the tents of Kedar, as the curtains of Solomon."
B. 1:6—". . . I am black."
C. 1:6—". . . my mother's children were angry with me; they made me the keeper of the vineyards; but mine own vineyard have I not kept."
D. 1:12—"While the king sitteth at his table, my spikenard sendeth forth the smell thereof."
E. 2:1—"I am the rose of Sharon, and the lily of the valleys."
F. 2:5—"Stay me with flagons, comfort me with apples: for I am sick of (with) love."

2. *THE TYPICAL IMPLICATION*

In the statements made by the Bride concerning herself, we find several typical implications. As we proceed to study the practical truths suggested in this division, we shall see that she becomes a type of the sinner, saved by grace; dead by nature, eternally alive by grace. She also typifies the believer who has seen his failure and makes humble confession, and returns to the place of testimony and faithful witness. Further, we shall see the value of the walk of separation from worldliness and sin.

3. *THE NEW TESTAMENT REVELATION*

A. Ephesians 5:8—"For ye were sometimes darkness, but now are ye light in the Lord."

B, C. I John 1:9—"If we confess our sins, he is faithful and just to forgive us our sins, and to cleanse us from all unrighteousness."

D. Ephesians 5:2—"And walk in love, as Christ also hath loved us, and hath given himself for us an offering and a sacrifice to God for a sweet smelling savour."

E. II Corinthians 5:17—"Therefore if any man be in Christ, he is a new creature: old things are passed away; behold, all things are become new."

F. John 17:26—"And I have declared unto them thy name, and will declare it: that the love wherewith thou hast loved me may be in them, and I in them."

4. *THE PRACTICAL APPLICATION*

A. 1:5—"I am black but comely . . . as the tents of Kedar, as the curtains of Solomon."

This twofold statement is not a contradiction, but a perfect description of the one who has been saved by grace through faith in Christ.

The Bride actually referred to her external appearance, for she had been blackened by the sun. But she has given us a beautiful type of our position by nature and our exalted position through grace.

Black, by nature; comely, through grace.

"Black . . . as the tents of Kedar," which were blackened by the sun. As our carnal nature, the flesh, can never be anything but black; the flesh can never be changed, or improved, or made acceptable to God.

"Comely . . . as the curtains of Solomon." We think of the veil in Solomon's Temple, a type of the holy humanity of our Lord Jesus. We need to remind ourselves that there is a "Man in the Glory," our risen, living Lord, and that it is His purpose that all believers are to be conformed to His image. "As we have borne the image of the earthy, we shall also bear the image of the heavenly" (I Cor. 15:49).

"We are *black* as sin in ourselves; whiter than snow in Christ."

The Psalmist writes in Psalm 139:14, ". . . I am fearfully and wonderfully made"; *fearfully* by nature, and wonderfully by grace. Our state was *fearful* before we were born again, but now, having passed from death unto life, our position, pathway, and prospect are *wonderful!*

The Apostle acknowledges, in Romans 7:18, "For I know that in me (that is, in my flesh,) dwelleth no good thing." As to the flesh, he was "black." But the first chapter of Ephesians reveals how "comely" he was "in Christ." And so with every child of God.

If we are to have a well-balanced conception of God's purposes for us for time and for eternity, we must see clearly both sides of this statement of the Bride concerning herself, "black, but comely." We must not fall into the disastrous practice of being so occupied with the "black," that we shall fail to rejoice that He sees us as "comely" in Himself. And, contrariwise, we must not forget what we were by nature, nor must we ignore the fact that the old nature, the flesh, still remains in us, along with the new nature, the Holy Spirit (Gal. 5:16, 17). This balanced regard for these facts will afford us a genuine appreciation for the grace of God, and will furnish a safeguard against spiritual conceit and dependence upon the energy of the flesh.

B. 1:6—". . . I am black."

C. 1:6—". . . my mother's children were angry with me; they made me the keeper of the vineyards; but mine own vineyard have I not kept."

Again the Bride refers to herself as "black," but here she omits the "but comely." There is a reason for this.

There have been several interesting and helpful interpretations of verse 6, each one bringing forth some decidedly practical truth along lines of warning as well as encouragement. But surely the indication is that the bride was placed in a position of responsibility, ". . . they made me the keeper of the vineyards," and there was failure, ". . . mine own vineyard have I not kept." It was not persecution which caused the failure, but the very prominence of her service led to neglect of the most important factor in her responsibility.

There is a great lesson here for those of us in that which we call "Christian service." We should remember that every born-again one is in "full-time" Christian service, the Christian doctor as well as the preacher in the pulpit; the Christian school teacher, as well as the foreign missionary; the Christian business man and woman, as well as the evangelist. If we are saved, and in the place of God's appointment, we are in the place of Christian service. The Bride, while taking the supervision over the interests of others, had neglected her own. So often it is the case with us that we become so busy in active service, in perfectly legitimate pursuits, reaching others with the gospel message, we neglect our own "vineyard," the sphere of our own personal lives. The very nature of the service, which puts us in the place of popularity and pre-eminence, may be the very snare which produces neglect of our spiritual needs. One has said, "It is easier to bear persecution than to bear popularity." The Apostle recognized the danger of this when he wrote to the Corinthians: ". . . I keep under my body, and bring it unto subjection: lest that by any means when I have preached to others, I myself should be a castaway (disapproved)" (I Cor. 9:27).

There is a danger, when we reach the place where we are "the keepers of other vineyards," that we shall feel that we do not need to *be kept.* Ah, there's the subtle working of the flesh and Satan. If that combination of adversaries can cause us to neglect the spiritual life and testimony of ourselves or our immediate families, a great victory has been gained for the enemy. The Bride was so overwhelmed with her failure that she acknowledged her "blackness," but did not mention, in this instance, her comeliness at all. But notice that she said, "the sun hath looked upon me (or scorched me)," *not* "hath burned me up." That is the fate of unbelievers (Matt. 13), never of the Bride. When sin enters the life and walk of the believer, *fellowship* with God is broken, but never the *relationship.* What is to be done? Instant confession (I John 1:9) and forgiveness, and restoration to the place of communion and usefulness.

We observe that the Bride speaks of her "mother's children"—fellow believers—being angry with her because she kept not *her own* vineyard. It is striking that they were not angry because she failed in keeping *their* vineyards, for she did not fail in that direction, but because she did not keep *her own.* It will be so with us who serve others, with faithfulness and fruitfulness, it may be, but who fail in our own spiritual responsibilities selfward and toward those of our immediate families. Our service to others will be forgotten if we, ourselves, fail. And the very ones to whom we have ministered most zealously, "our mother's children" will be our most severe critics. How closely we need to walk with the Lord, and how continuously we must lean upon Him, for strength, for power, and for personal blessing.

D. 1:12—"While the king sitteth at his table, my spikenard sendeth forth the smell thereof."

This is true worship. Worship is more than prayer; more than praise; more than thanksgiving. True worship is the overflow of the heart in love with the Lord Jesus.

In verse 3, the Bride has referred to the Bridgroom's "good ointments." He was sweet and fragrant to her. But *she* is sweet and fragrant to *Him*. And yet her "spikenard" is His gift from her. It is all of grace. The Psalmist expresses it in Psalm 23, "Thou anointest my head with oil; *my* cup *runneth over.*" There is never true worship until the cup runs over. The heart that worships is the overflowing heart. In the 14th of Mark, the story of Mary of Bethany, we see the spikenard *poured out* upon the Lord Jesus by the worshiper from a box *broken*. And the blessed result was that "the house was filled with the odour of the ointment" (Mark 14:3). Here is the main difference between prayer and worship. We approach *prayer* with empty vessels, asking our Father to fill them with heavenly supplies of His will and choosing. But we come to *worship* with vessels already full and running over. But O, my soul, thou must never forget that the very fulness is the gift of His grace. Yea, it is He, Himself!

Did you notice, particularly, that the Bride speaks of "her spikenard sending forth the smell thereof," "*while* the king sitteth at his table"? It was only while she was in close fellowship and communion with Him that there could be the sweetness of worship. He was in His proper place. There was no separation—nothing between. The table speaks of heavenly food, fellowship, supply, intimacy, and satisfaction. We remember also the Lord's table where, "as often as ye eat this bread and drink this cup, ye do show forth the Lord's death, till He come" (I Cor. 11:26). It is only upon the ground of the "blood *shed*" and the "broken body" of which *this* table speaks, that we may worship. The world and Christendom talk glibly of "Church Worship" and "Divine Worship Service," while knowing so little of genuine worship. There can be no worship acceptable to God the Father except it be centered in His beloved Son,

Jesus Christ. And it must be the Christ of Scripture, virgin-born, very God of very God, crucified, dead, buried, risen again out from among the dead in a body of flesh and bones (Luke 24:39), ascended to the throne of God, glorified, coming again visibly, personally, to rule and to reign. This is our Christ, and there is none other. *He* is the center of worship. Not some religious system, but Himself!

> "Lord Jesus Thou Who only art
> The endless source of purest joy
> Oh, come and fill this longing heart
> May nought but Thou my thoughts employ.
> Teach me on Thee to fix my eye,
> For none but Thou can satisfy.
>
> "The joys of earth can never fill
> The heart that's tasted of Thy love,
> No portion would I seek until
> I reign with Thee, my Lord above.
> When I shall gaze upon Thy face
> And know more fully of Thy grace.
>
> "Oh, what is all that earth can give—
> I'm called to share in God's own joy;
> Dead to the world, in Thee I live,
> In Thee I've bliss without alloy.
> Well may I earthly joys resign,
> 'All things' are mine; and I am Thine."

E. 2:1—"I am the rose of Sharon, and the lily of the valleys."

It is rather a common thing for some commentators, poets, and song writers to apply the titles in this verse to our Lord. It is fitting that every name and figure referring to that which is beautiful, be applied to the Lord Jesus. But it should be noted carefully that here the Bride applies these figures to herself, rather than to the Bridegroom. She looks into his face and dares to say, "*I* am the rose" (a blood red flower of Palestine); "*I* am the lily of the valleys."

Here is another illustration of "the grace of our Lord Jesus Christ." He places His own beauty upon the members of His body. He bestows His characteristics upon His people. Do we reveal them to others?

> "Can others see Jesus in you?
> Can others see Jesus in me?
> Oh, how shall the world know of Jesus,
> If it cannot see Jesus in me?"

The rose of Sharon is a blood red flower, and symbolizes, when the figure is applied to the believer, the life of beauty and sacrifice, beauty based upon sacrifice. "Except a corn of wheat fall into the ground and die, it abideth alone: but if it die, it bringeth forth much fruit" (John 12:24). We must live crucified lives, dead to sin, dead to the world, dead to self, dead to personal ambitions, then our lives will be beautiful and fruitful.

The lily of the valleys grows best in hidden places—not in the midst of the city—but in the quiet of the field. This suggests two lines of practical truth. First, the Christian, to be a delight to His Lord, must walk in the path of separation from sin and worldliness. "We cannot serve God and mammon." As a Chinese proverb has it: "When two men own a horse, it grows thin." The life pleasing to Christ is the life wholly devoted to Him and His interests. When we truly "fall in love" with Him, it no longer is a matter of "do I have to give up this, or must I sacrifice that pleasure?" But, rather, our first thought becomes, "how may I best please Him?" His lilies best grow in grace and in the knowledge of Him in the place of separation, of release from the bondage of the world and its lures.

And then, too, "the lily of the valleys" has a bit of comfort for those saints who serve in obscure places. We are apt to assume that God is more pleased with spectacular service than with secluded service. We are apt to feel that God rewards upon the basis of adding-machine totals, and that the one who can show statistics of large numbers of meetings conducted, of professed conversions, and crowds of listeners, will fare better at the judgment seat of Christ than the one who has served "in the shade," in the quiet place. Not so. Rewards will be given not for noise and commotion and display and numbers. Rewards (I Cor. 3) will be given for *faithfulness* in the place of His appointment. Mother in the home, bringing up the children to the glory of God; shut-in friend, conducting a ministry of prayer for God's people; pastor in the hard, small, unappreciative parish; rescue mission worker in the filth and squalor of the great city; take heart—lift up your heads, "lilies of the valleys," thy God is faithful to remember thy labor of love. If you are in the place to which He has assigned you, and are living the life of yielded service, you may count absolutely upon His blessing now and hereafter.

THE MASTER OF MY BOAT

I owned a little boat a while ago
And sailed a Morning Sea without a fear
And whither any breeze might fairly blow
I'd steer the little craft afar or near.

Mine was the boat, and mine the air.
And mine the sea, not mine, a care.

My boat became my place of nightly toil.
I sailed at sunset to the fishing ground.
At morn the boat was freighted with the spoil
That my all-conquering work and skill had found.

Mine was the boat, and mine the net.
And mine the skill, and power to get.

One day there passed along the silent shore,
While I my net was casting in the sea,
A man, who spoke as never man before;
I followed Him—new life began in me.

Mine was the boat, but His the voice.
And His the call, yet mine, the choice.

Once from His boat He taught the curious throng,
Then bade me let down nets out in the Sea;
I murmured, but obeyed, nor was it long
Before the catch amazed and humbled me.

His was the boat, and His the skill,
And His the catch, and His, my will.
—Joseph Addison Richards in "The Pilot."

F. 2:5—"Stay me with flagons, comfort me with apples: for I am sick of (with) love."

This language will be understood by the one who has been overwhelmed by love. The Bride is so completely captivated by the Bridegroom that she cannot think or speak of anything else. Someone has said, "The love of Christ satisfies, but never satiates the soul. While it satisfies to the full, it whets the appetite, and the Lord's delight is to give more abundantly. The Bride seeks to be sustained by the very love which has exhausted her."

Tread lightly here, fellow believer, for this indeed is holy ground.

Our fourth division provides for a study of

IV. WHAT THE BRIDEGROOM SAYS ABOUT HIMSELF

But it is interesting to see that here the Bridegroom and Bride are enjoying perfect communion, and while the Bride has much to say about the Bridegroom, and about herself made attractive to Him and to others by grace; and while the Bridegroom has a great deal to say concerning His Bride, He has no need to speak of Himself. The Bride, in perfect fellowship, does that for Him. She needs no verbal reminder of His beauty and loveliness. Her *heart* is responsive to Himself.

H. A. Ironside tells a story of a husband and father whose wife died and left only one child, a daughter, who was very dear to his heart. In those days of loneliness after the wife's death, he found his comfort in the beautiful girl. Every evening, when he came home from work, they would have their dinner together, and after the dishes had been put away, they would spend the evening together in the living room, greatly enjoying their fellowship together. As the holiday season approached, one evening the daughter said, "Father dear, you will excuse me tonight; I have some things to do upstairs. You can read while I am away." So the father sat alone. The next night the same thing happened, and night after night for two weeks the father was without the daughter's company. On Christmas morning the girl came to her father saying, "Merry Christmas, Father dear," and handed him a pair of beautiful slippers she had made for him. He expressed his appreciation, kissed her, and asked, "My darling, you made these yourself?" "Yes, Father." "Is that why I have not enjoyed your company for the past two weeks?" "Yes, that is my secret." "That is very sweet, daughter, but next time I would rather have *you* than anything you can make for me." The Lord Jesus wants *us*. Our heart's love means more to Him than anything we can *do* for Him. And the service that *grows* from communion is the choicest service.

BEYOND THE BRIGHTNESS OF THE SUN

Acts 22:11

I was journeying in the noontide,
When His light shone o'er my road;
And I saw Him in that glory—
Saw Him—Jesus, Son of God.

All around, in noonday splendour,
Earthly scenes lay fair and bright;
But my eyes no more behold them
For the glory of that light.

Others in the summer sunshine
Wearily may journey on,
I have seen a light from heaven,
Past the brightness of the sun—
Light that knows no cloud, no waning,
Light wherein I see His face
All His love's uncounted treasures,
All the riches of His grace:

All the wonders of His glory,
Deeper wonders of His love—
How for me He won, He keepeth
That high place in Heaven above;
Not a glimpse—the veil uplifted—
But within the veil to dwell,
Gazing on His Face for ever,
Hearing words unspeakable.

Marvel not that Christ in glory
All my inmost heart hath won;
Not a star to cheer my darkness,
But a light beyond the sun.
All below lies dark and shadowed,
Nothing there to claim my heart,
Save the lonely track of sorrow
Where of old He walked apart.

I have seen the Face of Jesus—
Tell me not of aught beside;
I have heard the Voice of Jesus—
All my soul is satisfied.
In the radiance of the glory
First I saw His blessed Face,
And for ever shall that glory
Be my home, my dwelling-place.

Section Two

SONG OF SOLOMON 2:8-3:4

I. WHAT THE BRIDE SAYS ABOUT THE BRIDE-GROOM

1. *THE DECLARATION*

A. 2:8—"The voice of my beloved!"

B. 2:8—". . . behold, he cometh leaping upon the mountains, skipping upon the hills."

C. 2:9—"My beloved is like a roe or a young hart: behold, he standeth behind our wall, he looketh forth at the windows, shewing himself through the lattice."

D. 2:16—"My beloved is mine, and I am his: he feedeth among the lilies."

2. *THE TYPICAL IMPLICATION*

There is a two-fold typical suggestion in these verses. First, there is the thought of the believer who has gone away from the Lord into a backslidden condition, in which there is broken fellowship with Him. We see this in the expressions of the Bride in this portion. We see also the path of return and restoration.

In the second place, the type is very clear of the believer in this world carrying on a testimony for Christ, possessed of the promise, "I will come again and receive you unto myself" (John 14:3), awaiting the call of the Heavenly Bridegroom, "Come up hither" (Rev. 4:1). Typically, the Lord's return is beautifully seen here, and, as we view it in a practical way, our hearts shall be warmed and encouraged.

3. *THE NEW TESTAMENT REVELATION*

A. John 18:37—". . . Every one that is of the truth heareth my voice."
Revelation 3:20—"Behold, I stand at the door, and knock: if any man hear my voice, and open the door, I will come in to him, and will sup with him, and he with me."

B. I Thessalonians 4:16, 17—"For the Lord himself shall descend from heaven with a shout, with the voice of the archangel, and with the trump of God: and the dead in Christ shall rise first: Then we which are alive and remain shall be caught up together with them in the clouds, to meet the Lord in the air: and so shall we ever be with the Lord."

C. Hebrews 9:24, 28—"For Christ is not entered into the holy places made with hands, which are the figures of the true; but into heaven itself, now to appear in the presence of God for us . . . And unto them that look for him shall he appear the second time without sin unto salvation."

D. John 17:10—"And all mine are thine, and thine are mine; and I am glorified in them."
John 14:20—". . . *ye* in me, and I in you."

4. *THE PRACTICAL APPLICATION*

A. 2:8—"The voice of my beloved!"

B. 2:8—". . . behold, he cometh leaping upon the mountains, skipping upon the hills."

The Bridegroom is absent from the Bride, and she longs for his return. In verses 4 to 7 of chapter 2, she is enjoying the most intimate, personal communion with him, but here, in verse 8, she can only speak of his "voice." It is one thing to hear our Lord's voice; it may be quite another to be enjoying Him.

There has been a break in the close fellowship. But it is only temporary and when her beloved knew of her desire, he came "leaping" and "skipping."

How gracious is our Lord in this regard. So many times, like the Bride, we "pay visits" to our Beloved. We rush into His presence, to pray, or to worship, and then, before we know it, we have rushed out again, and the continuity of communion is interrupted. The Bride had enjoyed fellowship—yes, but apparently as an occasional visitor, who had not yet learned that it is blessedly possible to enjoy continuous fellowship and enjoyment of her Beloved.

We become so busy with "things," and plans, and service, that many *good* things intercept the blessings which are found in the *best.* But just as a husband and wife, seated in a living room, may be occupied, each with his own separate and diverse duties, and yet conscious of one another in personal and sweet companionship, so may the believer live each moment of every day in a conscious, continuous sense of the Person and presence of his lovely Lord.

How quickly the Lord Jesus responds to the longing heart! Just one slight movement of the soul toward Him, and He comes "leaping" and "skipping."

The words "mountains" and "hills" contain gems of truth for us. So many times, in Christian experience, it seems as if mountains of difficulty, and hills of adverse circumstance stand in the way of our mutual progress and fellowship with our Lord. But He has promised, ". . . I will make all my mountains a way." Did you notice, "my mountains"? We discover, as we turn over the problem to Him, that the very obstacles and apparent hindrances become His highway by means of which He comes to us. How His presence glorifies the burdens of life! Paul the Apostle learned this grand lesson through his own experience with the "thorn in the flesh." Hear him say: "For this thing I besought the Lord thrice, that it might depart from me. And he said unto me, My grace is sufficient for thee: for my strength is made perfect in weakness. Most gladly therefore will I rather glory in my infirmities, that the power of Christ may rest upon me. Therefore, I take pleasure in infirmities, in reproaches, in necessities, in persecutions, in distresses for Christ's sake: for when I am weak then am I strong" (II Cor. 12:8-10). Such is the power and grace of our God, who can make the wrath of man to praise Him (Psalm 76:10), and who can make every mountain and hill—large burdens and small—a stepping stone to blessing and glory.

> C. 2:9—"My beloved is like a roe or a young hart: behold, he standeth behind our wall, he looketh forth at the windows, shewing himself through the lattice."

Three words are used here to describe the activity of the Bridegroom, "standeth," "looketh forth," "shewing himself." There is practical truth for us as we see the progress suggested.

We might think of these three expressions as suggestive of His incarnation, death, and resurrection. "Standing behind our wall" would remind us of His taking upon Himself the "likeness of sinful flesh" and identifying Himself with man in His incarnation. This is particularly significant since the word for "wall" in the original language of the Scripture is a word which suggests lumps of clay or earth. And it is *"our"* wall. He and we identified in this regard, that He clothed Himself with humanity. The words "Looketh forth at (or from) the windows" might be taken to signify His holy service among men here upon earth, while the last phrase "shewing himself" may well speak of His resurrection out from among the dead after His crucifixion and burial.

Again, we may look upon these three progressive expressions as indicative of His present ministry at the Father's right hand, and His coming again, first to receive His own unto Himself, and then in power and great glory to rule and to reign over the earth. "Standeth behind *our* wall" reminds us that as our representative and advocate with the Father (I John 2:1, 2), He is faithful and just to plead our case. The word "our" is precious, because we are completely identified with Him. The Father never sees us as apart from Him. We are, as believers, tied up in the same bundle of eternal life. When Stephen, martyred for the sake of his Christian testimony, looked up to heaven, "he saw the glory of God, and Jesus *standing* on the right hand of God." He is alive, and always ready to act on our behalf. The words "looketh forth at the windows" suggest that He is our faithful High Priest, who "ever liveth to make intercession for us" (Heb. 7:25). He is our advocate *when* we sin, but He is our High Priest to intercede for us to keep us from sin, and to guard and guide us in and through affliction. He "looketh forth" day and night. He never slumbers or sleeps. Nothing, however small, escapes His watchful eye and tender heart. The words "shewing Himself" surely tell us that "this same Jesus . . . shall so come in like manner" (Acts 1:10, 11). Praise God for the blessed hope of the Lord's return (Titus 2:11-14). Let the nations rage and evil seducers wax worse and worse; let the onslaughts of Satan be as fierce as they may; God is still on the throne, and His purposes in Christ can never fail in one single tiny detail. He is coming personally, visibly, bodily, right on time, powerfully, sovereignly, purposefully, graciously, judicially. Even so, come, Lord Jesus! Keep looking up!

D. 2:16—"My beloved is mine, and I am his: he feedeth among the lilies."

It is a wonderful thing to be able to say with absolute assurance, "Christ is mine, and I am His." So many of God's children seem afraid to say this with confidence. Some feel that it is a bit presumptuous for the Christian to speak definitely and possessively of this relationship to the Lord Jesus. But it should not be so. It is never presumptuous to believe God, and to trust His Word implicitly. The Scriptures are perfectly clear in declaring that the one who puts his faith where God has put his sins—on the Lord Jesus Christ, *has* eternal life, here and now. He may rest in that fact; he need never doubt it. "Verily, verily, I say unto you, He that heareth my word, and believeth on him that sent me, *hath* everlasting life, and shall not come into condemnation; but is passed from death unto life" (John 5:24); "He that *hath* the Son *hath* life" (I John 5:12); ". . . ye are Christ's" (I Cor. 3:23).

Three times in the Song of Solomon the Bride uses expressions similar to the one in this 16th verse. And it will be noted that there seems to be spiritual progress made as indicated by the wording of the three statements. Here she places first *her* possession of the Bridegroom, "My beloved is mine." Then she mentions his possession of her as secondary. In chapter 6, verse 3, she has made progress, for there she says, "I am my beloved's, and my beloved is mine." She puts His claim in first place, and her possession of Him as secondary. In chapter 7, verse 10, we again find a like expression, but there she is wholly occupied with the claims of the Bridegroom, for she says, "I am my beloved's, and his desire is toward me."

How important it is that we put Christ in first place.

As we think of our eternal salvation, we realize that He is the Author, the Originator of it (Heb. 5:9). As we think of our love for Him, we know that "We love him, because he first loved us" (I John 4:19). And we can say, "My beloved is mine," only because "I am my beloved's."

II. WHAT THE BRIDEGROOM SAYS ABOUT THE BRIDE

1. *THE DECLARATION*

A. 2:10—"Rise up, my love, my fair one, and come away."
2:13—". . . Arise, my love, my fair one, and come away."

B. 2:14—"O my dove, . . . in the clefts of the rock, in the secret (places) of the stairs . . ."

C. 2:14—". . . let me see thy countenance, let me hear thy voice; for sweet is thy voice, and thy countenance is comely."

D. 2:15—"Take us the foxes, the little foxes, that spoil the vines: for our vines have tender grapes."

2. *THE TYPICAL IMPLICATION*

In addition to the beautiful typical reference to the first phase of the Lord's return, the Rapture of the Church, in verses 10 to 13, we have in verse 14, the type of Christ, our Rock, our Fortress, being the Hiding Place for the dove, His people. Also in verse 14, we see not only the place of safety in Christ the Rock, but Christ the means of access into the Holiest Place, "the secret of the stairs." This suggests also spiritual progress—growth in grace and knowledge of our Lord Jesus Christ.

In the reference to the "little foxes" we have an illustration of the many "weights" and "sins" (Heb. 12:1) which enter the path of Christian experience and "spoil the vines" of sweet fellowship with our Lord, and hinder growth in grace.

3. *THE NEW TESTAMENT REVELATION*

A. I Corinthians 15:51, 52—"Behold, I shew you a mystery; We shall not all sleep, but we shall all be changed, in a moment, in the twinkling of an eye, at the last trump: for the trumpet shall sound, and the dead shall be raised incorruptible, and we shall be changed."

B. I Peter 2:3, 4—". . . the Lord is gracious. To whom coming, as unto a living stone, disallowed indeed of men, but chosen of God, and precious."
I Corinthians 10:4—". . . that Rock was Christ."
Romans 5:1, 2—". . . our Lord Jesus Christ: By whom also we have access . . ."

C. I Corinthians 13:12—"For now we see through a glass, darkly: but then face to face: now I know in part; but then shall I know even as also I am known."

D. Romans 12:1, 2—"I beseech you therefore, brethren, by the mercies of God, that ye present your bodies a living sacrifice, holy, acceptable unto God, which is your reasonable service. And be not conformed to this world: but be ye transformed by the renewing of your mind, that ye may prove what is that good, and acceptable, and perfect, will of God."

4. *THE PRACTICAL APPLICATION*

A. 2:10—"Rise up, my love, my fair one, and come away."
2:13—". . . Arise, my love, my fair one, and come away."

The obvious application of verses 10 to 13, with their beautiful imagery, is to the blessed truth of the Lord's return, first *for* His own loved ones, and then *with* His own subsequently, to rule and reign over the earth.

It is worthy of note here that the Bridegroom addresses his Bride as "my love, my fair one." No spot or blemish in her. As our Lord contemplates the reunion with His own, when He shall come for His church, He purposes to "present it to himself a glorious church, not having spot, or wrinkle, or any such thing; but that it should be holy and without blemish" (Eph. 5:27). But He does not wait until that day to rejoice in His love, His fair one. He sees us now, clothed with Himself, the Righteousness of God, and we are dear to Him. Oh, let us never take lower ground, practically, than the Lord provides for us.

While the call "come away," will be answered with tremendous power when the Lord descends from heaven, and we shall be caught up to meet Him in the air (I Thess. 4:13-18), as Lazarus answered the call when our Lord cried, "Lazarus, come forth" (John 11:43), there is a very practical application to us now, when He is saying to those who are members of His body, redeemed by His precious blood, saved by His grace, "come away"; come away from worldliness, from self-centered living, from desires of the flesh. "Come away" unto a life lived in perfect submission to Himself. The one who has come to know the blessedness of being a "bondslave of Christ" has entered into the life of the most glorious liberty.

As we think of our Lord coming again, it is well to remember that there may be considerable difference between "knowing the truth about the Lord's return," and really looking for the Lord. It is possible to be thoroughly familiar with all the scriptural details of prophecy; Israel's past, present and future; the Great Tribulation; the Millennium; the Rapture; and yet have little heart for the Lord Himself to come again. Let us be as those who ". . . wait (eagerly gazing) for his Son from heaven" (I Thess. 1:10).

B. 2:14—"O my dove, . . . in the clefts of the rock, in the secret (places) of the stairs . . ."

There is a vast difference between a dove and a rock. The one speaks of weakness and dependence, and the other of strength and stability. Christ is the Rock, which is the Hiding Place for all His "doves." What tenderness and loving concern are suggested by the figure used by the Bridegroom here. And what practical truth for us as we realize that our Rock was "cleft" for us, that we might be hidden eternally in Him.

"Rock of ages, cleft for me,
I have hid myself in Thee."

But there is another precious truth in verse 14. The Bridegroom speaks of "the secret of the stairs," (the word "places" is not in the original text). This suggests two things, free and full access into His presence; and growth in grace. "Stairs" are a means of access, and blessed are those "doves" who have learned the "secret" of these "stairs" of access. Growth in grace is accomplished just to the extent to which we use the stairs for continuous access into the presence of our Lord for prayer, worship and communion. The Psalmist tells us that "The secret of the Lord is with them that fear him" (Psalm 25:14). "Fear" in Old Testament usage, when applied to the believer's attitude toward God, does not imply horror or dread, but rather trust in God, with reverence and implicit confidence.

"In the secret of His presence,
How my soul delights to hide!
Oh, how precious are the lessons
Which I learn at Jesus' side!
Earthly cares can never vex me,
Neither trials lay me low;
For when Satan comes to tempt me,
To the secret place I go.

"Would you like to know the sweetness
Of the secret of the Lord?
Go and hide beneath His shadow:
This shall then be your reward;
And whene'er you leave the silence
Of that happy meeting place,
You must mind and bear the image
Of the Master in your face."

C. 2:14—". . . let me see thy countenance, let me hear thy voice; for sweet is thy voice, and thy countenance is comely."

There is a plaintive, almost pathetic note in this plea. Evidently the Bride had, in a measure, gotten away from the Bridegroom. The deep communion had been interrupted. And the Bridegroom longs for the restoration of that blessed fellowship. The *union* had not changed, but he pleads for a resumption of the *communion*. The *relationship* was the same, but the *fellowship* was lacking.

Have we heard our Lord say, "Let me see thy countenance, let me hear thy voice," and have we turned away from His plea? Notice that He asks first to see the *countenance,* even before He asks to hear the *voice*—a reminder that there is something higher than prayer in connection with our relationship to Christ. When He chose His disciples, it was first "that they should be with Him" (Mark 3:14). What grace, that He finds it in His heart to say unto us, "sweet is thy voice, and thy countenance is comely." Surely it will take the ages of eternity to unfold the story of His marvelous, infinite, matchless grace.

D. 2:15—"Take us the foxes, the little foxes, that spoil the vines: for our vines have tender grapes."

In verse 6 of the first chapter, the Bride had told of being "made the keeper of the vineyards." As such she realized the danger to the vines afforded by the "little foxes." Traps must be set to catch them lest they damage the "tender grapes." Now the Bridegroom uses the figure as an illustration of the dangers to spiritual life. Again we see how graciously the Bridegroom identifies himself with the Bride in the care of the vineyard, "take *us* the foxes"; "for *our* vines have tender grapes."

Our Lord exhorts us to *"watch* and pray" (Matt. 26:41). It is vital that we pray, but we must not neglect the "watch." It is the *watching* which corresponds with the thought in verse 15. When things are discovered in the life and walk which jeopardize and hinder spiritual growth and fellowship, they are to be judged and confessed. "For if we would judge ourselves, we should not be judged. But when we are judged, we are chastened of the Lord, that we should not be condemned with the world" (I Cor. 11:31, 32).

Some of the "little foxes that spoil the vines" are pride, envy, self-exultation, spiritual laziness, critical spirit, prayerlessness, evil speaking, jealousy, and many more. If we are honest with ourselves, we shall know just where we must "set the traps." It is not always the great, outbreaking sins which spoil the vines. They are more easily recognized and catalogued as sins. But the "little foxes" often pass, in our estimation, for "temperamental pecularities," or "unavoidable weakness," or "unfortunate tendencies," and thus we are apt to neglect to be vigilant and thorough in "setting traps." Because "our vines have tender grapes," let us trust the Holy Spirit to give us extreme sensitivity toward "little foxes."

III. WHAT THE BRIDE SAYS ABOUT HERSELF

1. *THE DECLARATION*

A. 3:1—"By night on my bed I sought him whom my soul loveth: I sought him, but I found him not."

3:2—"I will rise now, and go about the city in the streets, and in the broad ways I will seek him whom my soul loveth: I sought him, but I found him not."

3:3—"The watchmen that go about the city found me: to whom I said, Saw ye him whom my soul loveth?"

3:4—"It was but a little that I passed from them, but I found him whom my soul loveth: I held him, and would not let him go until I had brought him into my mother's house, and into the chamber of her that conceived me."

2. *THE TYPICAL IMPLICATION*

Certainly in this passage, the typical implication is clear, for it furnishes an illustration of the child of God, who, being in a backslidden state, has been awakened, by the gracious Person and work of the Holy Spirit, to a consciousness of being apart from real fellowship with Christ, and being restored again, not merely to a *state* of fellowship, but to Himself.

Just a word here as to that which is intended by the phrase "the typical implication." Some readers will not be wholly in agreement with a statement that every part of this Song of Songs provides some distinct *type,* although the Apostle, in I Corinthians 10:11, clearly declares, "Now all these things happened unto them (referring to Old Testament events) for ensamples, (or, as types), and they are written for *our* admonition, upon whom the ends of the world (ages) are come." Call them what you will, symbols, figures, illustrations, they are beautifully clear pictures of these unspeakably precious truths revealed in the New Testament.

We see in verses 1 to 4 also a picture of the nation of Israel, God's Covenant people, once in fellowship with Jehovah, but now scattered throughout the Gentile nations, judicially blinded because of rejection of their Messiah, but one glorious day "they shall look upon Him whom they have pierced, and they shall mourn for Him, as one mourneth for his only son" (Zech. 12:10). There shall be restoration and renewed communion, fruitfulness and blessing.

3. *THE NEW TESTAMENT REVELATION*

A. James 4:8—"Draw nigh to God, and he will draw nigh to you."

Jude 3—". . . earnestly contend for the faith which was once (for all) delivered unto the saints."

Colossians 3:1—"If ye then be risen with Christ, seek those things which are above where Christ sitteth on the right hand of God."

I John 1:8-10—"If we say that we have no sin, we deceive ourselves, and the truth is not in us. If we confess our sins he is faithful and just to forgive us our sins, and to cleanse us from all unrighteousness. If we say that we have not sinned, we make him a liar, and his word is not in us."

Ephesians 5:14-16—"... Awake thou that sleepest, and arise from the dead, and Christ shall give thee light. See then that ye walk circumspectly, not as fools, but as wise, Redeeming the time, because the days are evil."

4. *THE PRACTICAL APPLICATION*

Four times, in these verses, the Bride refers to the Bridegroom as "him whom my soul loveth." And in the fourfold use of this phrase, we learn some things about the Bride (for she is telling her own experiences here), and some practical lessons for ourselves as well.

First, in verse 1, "By night on my bed I sought *him whom my soul loveth.*" The Bride had gone to bed, but she could neither sleep nor rest, for she had learned what multitudes of other Christians had learned in the centuries since, that there is no true peace or rest for the soul and spirit apart from the heavenly Bridegroom, Christ.

And yet, in verse 1, she had not learned that "on her bed" was not the place to seek Him. In chapter 2, verses 10 and 13, the Beloved twice had asked her to "rise up," but here we find her, not yet obedient to His command, and yet *seeking* Him. What a lesson for us. There can be no real fellowship and communion between the believer and his Lord apart from complete obedience. Things must be done in God's way, if we are to have God's blessing. So many times we are inclined to take the course of expediency or convenience to ourselves, and then wonder why we are without the Lord's blessing, and a sense of His presence.

In chapter 2 of Luke's Gospel, verses 41 to 52, is found

the story of Jesus and His parents attending the feast of the passover at Jerusalem. After the feast days were completed, the parents started on their homeward journey, but Jesus, who was twelve years old at the time, tarried behind in Jerusalem. Joseph and Mary didn't miss Him until they had gone a whole day's journey toward home. When they discovered His absence, what did they do? They immediately went back to the temple in Jerusalem and found Him, *just where they had left Him.* They *sought* Him, and *found* Him.

Friend, if you have been walking the path of sin, or carelessness, or indifference, and, even though a child of God, have been out of fellowship with him and His people, do not remain "on the bed" of disobedience, or lethargy, but "rise up," return to the place where *you left the Lord,* and there you will find Him, waiting to be gracious, eager to forgive when you confess your sin, and merciful to restore you to His bosom of compassion and love.

Second, in verse 2, we find the phrase again, "I will rise now, and go about the city in the streets, and in the broad ways I will seek *him whom my soul loveth*: I sought him, but I found him not."

Now she is making some progress, at least as concerns her own attitude. But again she fails to find him. We see the reason for her failure in the words "the city, in the streets, and in the broad ways." Throughout the Song of Solomon, the city seems to stand for world conformity, and the words and phrases which characterize the Bridegroom's haunts are "lilies," "the shepherd's tents," "grass," "mountains," "hills," "field," "garden," "beds of spices." There is no fragrance in the city. There is noise, business, confusion, work, but little rest to attract the weary soul and body. That is found in the country, the fields, the gardens.

When we say "the city" we are reminded of man's efforts,

the best that he can do. It has attractiveness of a sort, but nothing like God's handiwork. Here is the difference between the "works of the flesh" (Gal. 5:19-21), noisy, much energy, confusion, bitterness, clamor, and "the fruit of the Spirit" (Gal. 5:22, 23), like a garden, fruitful, fragrant, silently growing, God's work.

If we would find Christ in this sense of enjoying the fullest communion with Him, it must not be through fleshly activity "in the city,"—ritualism, ecclesiasticism, pomp and display, loud cryings and agonizing; but rather through yieldedness to the Holy Spirit, allowing Him to make real to us the Person of the Lord Jesus in all His beauty and strength.

The third appearance of this phrase is in verse 3, where the watchmen in the city find the Bride, and she asks them, "Saw ye Him whom my soul loveth?"

There is a lovely thought associated with these "watchmen." It will be noted that while the Bride was conducting her search for the Bridegroom, the watchmen *found her.* It is the duty of watchmen to care for the safety and convenience of the inhabitants, to give direction to those who were in need of counsel and help. It is our privilege and responsibility, as Christians, to be "watchmen" in the sense of giving assistance and encouragement to those who need the Lord and are seeking Him, as well as giving the gospel to those who are unsaved and need to be born again. Was not this in the mind of the Apostle when he wrote, "Bear ye one another's burdens, and so fulfill the law of Christ" (Gal. 6:2)?

We are not told whether these watchmen to whom the Bride spoke gave her any help. It is possible that they did. In any event, her search was finally rewarded, for in verse 4, we find her saying, "It was but a little that I passed from them, but I found *him whom my soul loveth*: I held him, and would not let him go, until I had brought him into my mother's house, and into the chamber of her that conceived me."

The Lord Jesus loves to be sought by His own. The unsaved one does not seek the Lord. It is a mistake to ask one who has not accepted Christ as Saviour to "seek the Lord." Paul clearly declares in Romans 3:11 ". . . there is none that seeketh after God." The unsaved one hears the gospel of the grace of God, "which is the power of God unto salvation" (Rom. 1:16), and hearing ". . . how that Christ died for our sins according to the scriptures; And that he was buried, and that he rose again the third day according to the scriptures" (I Cor. 15:3, 4), he believes, receives Christ, and is born again into the family of God.

There is an illustration of "divine coquetry" in Luke 24, where the risen Christ met the two discouraged disciples on the road to Emmaus. They were sad because they were in error as to God's purposes in the Person and work of Christ. And while they walked, "Jesus, himself, drew near, and went with him" (Luke 24:15). After further conversation but before they recognized the Lord, ". . . they drew nigh unto the village, whither they went: *and he made as though he would have gone further*. But they constrained him, saying, Abide with us: for it is toward evening, and the day is far spent. And he went in to tarry with them." (vss. 28, 29). There is a beautiful touch in the phrase ". . . He made as though he would have gone further." Do you recall the "courting days," when, on Sunday evening, after church, you would walk home with the one of your choice? You would walk slowly, oh, so slowly, that the enjoyment of the occasion might be prolonged as much as possible. And then, upon reaching the front door of the young lady's home, *he* would say, rather reluctantly, and secretly hopeful, "Well, I suppose I should be going now." He "made" as though he would go home. And then *she* would respond, oh, sweet words, "Oh, it isn't late; come in for a while, will you?" Sure, he would. The invitation was just what *he* was waiting and hoping for.

The Bride found her Beloved, but in her statement in the last half of verse 4, she indicates that she has not yet learned all that she needs to learn, either about *herself* or her lover. Notice that she emphatically says, "I held him, and would not let him go." As if he *wanted* to go.

Our blessed Lord has promised, "I will never leave thee nor forsake thee" (Heb. 13:5; Matt. 28:20). *We* cannot hold *Him,* but *He* holds *us.* We are in His hand (John 10:27-31) and kept by His power (I Pet. 1:5).

> "I hold not the Rock,
> But the Rock holds me."

Some would urge the Christian to "hold on to Christ" or to "hang on to salvation" as if we had the power or ability to do so. No, His "strength is made perfect in weakness" (II Cor. 12:9), and the secret of fruitfulness and blessing in the Christian life is in the realization that our relationship to God in Christ is one of *birth,* the new birth, and the *relationship* and *position* can never be rescinded or altered. We are saved by grace, and kept by grace, every step of the way. We who have received Christ *have eternal life now,* just as truly as we shall have it ten million years from now.

The key words of this relationship, in its practical outworking, are the words found often in the Epistles of Paul; "know," "reckon," "yield," and "let." He is the One "who is able to do exceeding abundantly above all that we ask or think" (Eph. 3:20).

Section Three

SONG OF SOLOMON 3:6-5:1

I. WHAT THE BRIDE SAYS ABOUT THE BRIDEGROOM

1. *THE DECLARATION*

A. 3:6—". . . cometh out of the wilderness like pillars of smoke, perfumed with myrrh and frankincense, with all the powders of the merchant."

B. 3:7, 8—"Behold his bed (couch) . . . threescore valiant men are about it. They all hold swords, being expert in war: every man hath his sword upon his thigh . . ."

C. 3:9-11—"King Solomon made himself a chariot of the wood of Lebanon . . . pillars . . . of silver . . . bottom . . . of gold, the covering of it of purple, the midst thereof being paved with love . . . behold King Solomon with the crown . . ."

D. 4:16—"Let my beloved come into his garden, and eat his pleasant fruits."

2. *THE TYPICAL IMPLICATION*

In verses 6 to 11 we have a clear, typical picture—prophetically—of Christ, the Heavenly Bridegroom, united with His Bride, the Church, coming back to the earth, to gather His wandering ones of national Israel, restoring them to "the land" which was promised to them unconditionally so many centuries ago.

The Church is to be "caught up . . . to meet the Lord in the air" (I Thess. 4:13-18). This promise was never made to Israel. Her prospect is earthly; the destiny of the Church is heavenly. And when Christ comes again as King, His Bride, the Church, will be with Him, to share His judgments and His reign. Therefore Christ, as King, goes to where Israel is. The prophetic Scriptures tell us that the Messiah reveals Himself to Israel "in the wilderness," for we read in Hosea 2, "I will allure her, and bring her into the wilderness, and speak comfortably unto her." Also Revelation 12:14, "And to the woman (the remnant of Israel) were given two wings of a great eagle, that she might fly into the wilderness, into her place, where she is nourished for a time, and times, and half a time, from the face of the serpent."

We find a similar prophetic and typical picture of Christ as Messiah and King in Psalm 45. It is one of the most instructive and inspiring portions looking forward to the day of His glorious appearing and rule.

It is well for us to remember that Christ is never called "the King of the Church." By His grace, we are brought into a higher relationship than that of the subjects of the King. We enjoy the place of a Bride in the affections and care and purposes of the Bridegroom. If we habitually recognize the high calling which is ours in Christ Jesus (Phil. 3:14) we shall habitually walk in a path consistent with it.

3. *THE NEW TESTAMENT REVELATION*

A. Hebrews 8:10-12—"For this is the covenant that I will make with the house of Israel after those days, saith the Lord; I will put my laws into their mind, and write them in their hearts: and I will be to them a God, and they shall be to me a people.

And they shall not teach every man his neighbor, and every man his brother, saying, Know the Lord: for all shall know me, from the least to the greatest.

For I will be merciful to their unrighteousness, and their sins and their iniquities will I remember no more."

B. II Thessalonians 1:7-10—". . . the Lord Jesus shall be revealed from heaven with his mighty angels, In flaming fire taking vengeance on them that know not God, and that obey not the gospel of our Lord Jesus Christ: Who shall be punished with everlasting destruction from the presence of the Lord, and from the glory of his power; When he shall come to be glorified in his saints . . ."

C. I Peter 1:18, 19—"Forasmuch as ye know that ye were not redeemed with corruptible things, as silver and gold . . . But with the precious blood of Christ, as of a lamb without blemish and without spot."

John 1:1—"In the beginning was the Word, and the Word was with God, and the Word was God."

I Timothy 6:14, 15—". . . the appearing of the Lord Jesus Christ: Which in his times he shall shew, who is the blessed and only Potentate, the King of kings, and Lord of lords."

John 3:16—"For God so loved the world, that he gave his only begotten Son, that whosoever believeth in him should not perish, but have everlasting life."

4. *THE PRACTICAL APPLICATION*

A. 3:6-8—". . . cometh out of the wilderness like pillars of smoke, perfumed with myrrh and frankincense, with all powders of the merchant."

B. 3:7—"Behold his bed (couch) . . . threescore valiant men are about it. They all hold swords, being expert in war: every man hath his sword upon his thigh . . ."

The Bride is now in the enjoyment of sweet communion with the Bridegroom, after their separation and subsequent restoration. And immediately she is occupied with the beauty and fragrance of his Person (v.6). That is the focal point of attractiveness to the believer—it is Christ Himself. Not first His power, His diety, His eternal uncreated existence—as vital and true as these things are—but Himself.

And then, since she is now in fellowship with him, she is permitted to share a view of his Kingly splendor, and the glories of his reign. King Solomon is a type of Christ as King, and so these references in verses 6 to 11 have particular significance for us. The Lord Jesus Himself made several references to Solomon (Matt. 6:29; 12:42). The name "Solomon" means "Peaceable." Christ is the Prince of Peace. There will be world peace when He returns, but not until then.

There is a most practical thought for us in the fact that when the Bride saw her Beloved during this time of perfect communion and fellowship, she saw *other men* with him. When we are in closest fellowship with our Lord, we are in closest fellowship with other believers. We are then most conscious of their needs, burdens, joys and sorrows. We are most aware also of the unsaved people all about us, and are the most desirous of reaching them with the message of salvation. "The love of God . . . shed abroad in our hearts by the Holy Spirit" (Rom. 5:5) not only flows *upward* toward God, but *outward* toward others.

C. 3:9-11—"King Solomon made himself a chariot of the wood of Lebanon . . . pillars thereof of

> silver . . . bottom thereof of gold, the covering of it of purple, the midst thereof being paved with love . . . behold king Solomon with the crown . . ."

These verses are rich in typical and practical truth. There are several key words of great depth of meaning, "made himself," "wood of Lebanon," "pillars," "silver," "gold," "purple," "paved with gold," "crown."

The "chariot" is the King's royal carriage. He "made himself a chariot." The "wood of Lebanon" is the cedar, and is typical of fragrance and permanence. We are reminded thus of the incarnation, when God the Son, "made Himself of no reputation" (Phil. 2:7), and "came in the likeness of sinful flesh" (Rom. 8:3). "Wood" in Scripture, as applied to our Lord, is typical of His humanity, and the "cedar wood" tells us, in figure, that He, in His humanity, as in His diety, is incorruptible, and absolutely holy. He "made *himself* a chariot." Christ completes the work for His people. He invites us to enter into the practical enjoyment of that which He has done, and is now doing, and shall yet do for us.

"Pillars" speak of strength, and "silver" is always typical of redemption. Our Lord, Who *is* our Strength (Psalm 18:2) has redeemed us by His own precious blood.

"Gold" stands for Diety and divine righteousness. Christ is God, and He is "the Righteousness of God" (Rom. 3:21; I Cor. 1:30). God's Righteousness, imputed unto us who believe, is not merely an attitude, but a Person. He is "made unto us righteousness."

"Purple" is the color of royalty. Christ, in Scripture, is seen in three offices, those of Prophet, Priest, and King. He does not execute the functions of those offices simultaneously, but consecutively. As Prophet He came to this earth, by way of Bethlehem, went about doing good, presented Himself as Messiah to Israel, preached the Gospel of the Kingdom, went to the cross, shedding His own precious blood, that He might "bear our sins in his own body" (I Pet. 2:24). As Priest, He is now at the right hand of the throne of God, in a body of flesh and bones, making intercession for us (Heb. 4:14; 7:25). As King He shall come again, in power and great glory, to rule and reign in judgment and righteousness. Our salvation is in three tenses—salvation *past,* deliverance from the *penalty* of sin, Christ as Prophet; salvation *present,* deliverance from the *power* of sin, Christ as Priest; salvation *future,* deliverance from the *presence* of sin, Christ as King.

We remember also I Peter 2:9, ". . . ye are . . . a *royal* priesthood"; and Revelation 1:5,6, "Jesus Christ . . . hath made *us* kings and priests unto God." We shall reign with Him. All purposes and plans involving the Lord Jesus for all eternity include us who are redeemed, and members of His Body. Nothing He shall do shall be done apart from ourselves. Wondrous grace!

"Paved with love" implies that love is the foundation of all His gracious purposes. "God *is* love." "God *so* loved." His love as manifested in Christ furnishes the divine highway for His plan for the Jew, the Gentile, and the Church of God.

When we put all the words of this portion together, it tells a lovely story: Our *Solomon,* Christ Jesus, humbled *Himself,* left the glory which He had with the Father from all eternity, clothed Himself with the *cedar wood* of holy humanity, that He might establish the *pillars of silver* for our redemption, to make us "partakers of the divine nature" (II Pet. 1:4), a "royal priesthood" *(gold and purple).* All of this because of His eternal *love* for us. Now behold our Lord *"crowned* with glory and honour" (Heb. 2:9).

"Resplendent Bridegroom, venerated Lord!
Prince of all kings! Eternal Sovereign!
Rich, wise, and royal, Solomon indeed!
Of Thee—exclusively of Thee and Thine—

> This Song of Songs, this hallowed Canticle!
> Its thrilling tones, too little understood,
> Treat not of earth's affections, but in type,
> And shadowing forth of holy mysteries,
> It speaks of the Beloved—the King of Peace—
> Salem's great Architect; it speaks of One
> Who builds a temple to Jehovah's praise,
> Which the descending glory shall pervade
> And fill eternally—It speaks of One
> Whose enemies shall all be clothed with shame,
> While on Himself the universal crown
> For ever radiates—It speaks of One
> At whose high throne of peace and equity
> Prayer shall be made, and happy nations bend,
> Rejoicing in His sway of righteousness."

D. 4:16 (last sentence)—". . . Let my beloved come into his garden, and eat his pleasant fruits."

We shall consider this statement in connection with subdivision II.

II. WHAT THE BRIDEGROOM SAYS ABOUT THE BRIDE

1. *THE DECLARATION*

A. 4:1—"Behold, thou art fair, my love; behold, thou art fair."

4:7—"Thou art all fair, my love; there is no spot in thee."

B. 4:1—". . . thou hast doves' eyes within thy locks."

C. 4:1—". . . thy hair is as a flock of goats, that appear from Mount Gilead."

D. 4:2—"Thy teeth are like a flock of sheep that are even shorn, which came up from the washing, whereof every one bear twins, and none is barren among them."

E. 4:3—"Thy lips are like a thread of scarlet, and thy speech is comely."

F. 4:3—". . . thy temples are like a piece of a pomegranate within thy locks."

G. 4:4—"Thy neck is like the tower of David builded for an armoury, whereon there hang a thousand bucklers, all shields of mighty men."

H. 4:5—"Thy two breasts are like two young roes that are twins, which feed among the lilies."

I. 4:8—"Come with me from Lebanon . . . look from the top of Amana, from the top of Shenir and Hermon, from the lions' dens, from the mountains of the leopards."

J. 4:9—"Thou hast ravished my heart, my sister."

K. 4:10—". . . how much better is thy love than wine!"

L. 4:11—". . . the smell of thy garments is like the smell of Lebanon."

M. 4:12-16—"A garden inclosed is my sister, my spouse; a spring shut up, a fountain sealed.

Thy plants are an orchard of pomegranates, with pleasant fruits; camphire, with spikenard,

Spikenard and saffron; calamus and cinnamon, with all trees of frankincense; myrrh and aloes, with all the chief spices:

A fountain of gardens, a well of living waters, and streams from Lebanon.

Awake, O north wind; and come, thou south; blow upon my garden, that the spices thereof may flow out . . ."

2. *THE TYPICAL IMPLICATION*

Truly we tread here upon holy ground, for we have, in language of exquisite beauty, the Bridegroom's estimate of the Bride, in all the attractiveness of her person.

Again we see—with limited vision, of course, because of these finite, sin-blotted minds of ours—how precious we are to Christ. He clothes us with the perfect, spotless Righteousness of God—Christ Himself—and then revels in our beauty. It is not a beauty of the flesh, mind you, for "they that are in the flesh, cannot please God" (Rom. 8:8). It may be very beautiful flesh, naturally, and cultured, educated, talented flesh, but there is nothing in the flesh pleasing to God. We must learn that at the cross God put the flesh forever out of His sight. He will not accept anything offered unto Him in or by the flesh. But, oh, the marvel of His grace! We now can say, "The beauty of the Lord our God is upon us" (Psalm 90:17).

After the Bridegroom has spoken generally of the beauty of his Bride, he mentions seven distinct personal features in which he particularly delights. He speaks of the *eyes,* the *hair,* the *teeth,* the *lips,* the *temples,* the *neck,* and the *breasts.* The number "seven" in Scripture signifies divine fulness and completeness. Thus this sevenfold reference to the features of the Bride, indicates that to him she is the fulness of perfection and beauty. As we study the seven features separately, we shall find practical instruction for our hearts.

In verses 12 to 16, we find a type of the believer as a garden. A garden exists for the purpose of bearing fruit. God could have taken us home to heaven the moment we were saved, had He desired to do so. But He left us here to bear fruit. The words of our Lord in John 15:16 come to mind, "Ye have not chosen me, but I have chosen you, and ordained you, that ye should go and *bring forth fruit,* and that your fruit should remain . . ."

3. *THE NEW TESTAMENT REVELATION*

A. John 17:26—"And I have declared unto them thy name, and will declare it: that the love wherewith thou hast loved me may be in them, and I in them."

B. Matthew 6:22—"The light of the body is the eye: if therefore thine eye be single, thy whole body shall be full of light."

C. John 12:3—"Then took Mary a pound of ointment of spikenard, very costly, and anointed the feet of Jesus, and wiped his feet with her hair: and the house was filled with the odour of the ointment."

D. Titus 3:2—". . . speak evil of no man."

E. Titus 2:8—"Sound speech, that cannot be condemned; that he that is of the contrary part may be ashamed, having no evil thing to say of you."

F. I Peter 3:3, 4—"Whose adorning . . . let it be the hidden man of the heart, in that which is not corruptible, even the ornament of a meek and quiet spirit, which is in the sight of God of great price."

G. II Timothy 2:3—"Thou therefore endure hardness, as a good soldier of Jesus Christ."

H. Ephesians 6:11, 14—"Put on the whole armour of God . . . having on the breastplate of righteousness."

I. Revelation 22:17—"And the Spirit and the bride say, Come. And let him that heareth say, Come. And let him that is athirst come. And whosoever will, let him take the water of life freely."

M. John 7:37-39—"In the last day, that great day of the feast, Jesus stood and cried, saying, If any man thirst, let him come unto me, and drink.

He that believeth on me, as the scripture hath said, out of his belly (innermost being) shall flow rivers of living water.

But this spake he of the Spirit, which they that believe on him should receive; for the Holy Spirit was not yet given; because that Jesus was not yet glorified."

4. *THE PRACTICAL APPLICATION*

A. 4:1—"Behold, thou art fair, my love; behold, thou art fair."

4:7—"Thou art all fair, my love; there is no spot in thee."

B. 4:1—". . . thou hast doves' *eyes* within thy locks."

As the Bridegroom looks upon the Bride, and sees absolute, spotless perfection, he enumerates seven features in which he takes particular delight.

As our blessed Lord looks upon His redeemed, blood-bought people, He sees us as we shall be one day, conformed to His image, "not having spot, or wrinkle, or any such thing" (Eph. 5:27). May we not see, in this sevenfold tribute to the Bride, references to those characteristics in the believer, which are a special delight to the Lord Jesus?

The first reference is to the *eyes*. And he calls them "doves' eyes." The dove was a ceremonially clean bird, used in sacrifice, and was a symbol of harmlessness, purity, and tenderness. The eye is referred to in Scripture in connection with spiritual discernment and understanding. As our Lord said, in Matthew 6:22, "The light of the body is the eye: if therefore thine eye be single, thy whole body shall be full of light." One Bible scholar has pointed out that the dove has a wonderful power of *distant* vision. "When it is taken far from home, and released from its cage, it will ascend high into the air, until it has discovered the way back; then it flies straight and rapidly home. And so we, having seen by faith the risen Jesus, may forget the things that are behind, and press on to those that are before. Christ, Himself, is our mark—but the 'mark' must be seen before we can take our aim. First, fix thine eye on the risen, exalted Man in Glory."

> C. 4:1—". . . thy *hair* is as a flock of goats, that appear from Mount Gilead."

Our first thought here is of Paul's reference to woman's hair being a glory to her (I Cor. 11:15). It is a mark of subjection to authority.

But there may be also the reference to the long hair of the Nazarite (Numbers 6) which was the visible sign of separation unto God, and his willingness to bear scorn and reproach for the Lord's sake. In this spirit of subjection and separation, when found in His people, our Lord greatly delights.

> D. 4:2—"Thy *teeth* are like a flock of sheep that are even shorn, which come up from the washing, whereof every one bear twins, and none is barren among them."

How beautiful to the Lord are clean, even, sets of spiritual teeth. They are vital to mastication of spiritual food. It is sad, but true, that there are a number of toothless Christians. It is not uncommon to hear a believer say, "I wonder what he can find so fascinating about reading and studying the Bible so much of the time. I don't seem to get much out of mine." The trouble is that that one "bolts his food" instead of properly chewing it. Meditating upon the Word of God is the key to real enjoyment of it. The Apostle exhorts Timothy, "Meditate upon these things; give thyself wholly to them: that thy profiting may appear to all" (I Tim. 4:15).

E. 4:3—"Thy *lips* are like a thread of scarlet, and thy speech is comely."

There is no artificial "lip stick" involved in this tribute. But the "scarlet" speaks of the "scarlet line of sacrifice" which runs straight through the Holy Scriptures from Genesis to Revelation. It is the shed blood of the Lamb of God. In these days, many are ridiculing the "precious blood," some are ignoring it, others are telling us that it is not adequate to atone for sin, and that something of our own works and effort must be added to it. But it still is God's only way of propitiation. "The blood can never lose its power." "God forbid that I should glory, save in the cross of our Lord Jesus Christ" (Gal. 6:14). Our "speech is comely" when we confess that our eternal salvation rests upon that atoning blood, by which we draw nigh to God.

Throughout eternity we shall have "lips like a thread of scarlet," for we shall sing "Unto him that loved us, and washed us from our sins in his own blood" (Rev. 1:5).

F. 4:3—". . . thy *temples* are like a piece of a pomegranate within thy locks."

We note here that the *temples* of the Bride—the place of *thought*—are likened to a "piece," a broken part, of a pomegranate. The fruit is delicious to the taste, and when broken is a bright red color, mixed with white. This may suggest modesty, or blushing, and reminds us of I Peter 3:3, 4, "Whose adorning . . . let it be the hidden man of the heart, in that which is not corruptible, even the ornament of a meek and quiet spirit, which is in the sight of God of great price."

Our *temples* are a delight to the Lord when, in meekness and true humility, our thoughts are devoted to Him.

G. 4:4—"Thy *neck* is like the tower of David builded for an armoury, whereon there hang a thousand bucklers, all shields of mighty men."

The practical application of this verse is surely obvious, for "the tower of David" is the place of strength and defense. The neck, when normal, holds the head erect, and we may look boldly forward into the face of any enemy, for we have "put on the whole armour of God," and can "be strong in the Lord, and in the power of his might" (Eph. 6:10, 11).

Let us not be "stiff-necked," as was Israel, but rejoice to wear the yoke of the Lord Jesus (Matt. 11:29, 30), confident that we can do all things through Christ which strengtheneth us (Phil. 4:13).

H. 4:5—"Thy two *breasts* are like two young roes that are twins, which feed among the lilies."

The *breast* suggests the place of affection. The word "twins" brings to mind the exhortation in I Thessalonians 5:8, ". . . putting on the breastplate of *faith* and *love,"* the *twins* of Christian blessing and growth. Believing Him, trusting Him, and loving Him.

I. 4:8—"Come with me from Lebanon . . . look from the top of Amana, from the top of Shenir and Hermon, from the lions' dens, from the mountains of the leopards."

The mountain is the place of worldly power and glory, and because of that fact, there is danger to the child of God on the mountain. There are lions and leopards there, who crouch subtly and slyly to take the Christian unaware.

The Lord Jesus is saying to His own that sweet word "Come." It is a difficult word to define. It means "come"—that's all. See that little babe just learning to walk; he doesn't understand the meaning of many words. But when Mother stretches forth her arms to him and says, "Come," he knows what that means. So our Lord uses that lovely word many times throughout the Scriptures:

In John 11:43 is "Come FORTH"—the "come" of REGENERATION.

In Luke 19:5 is "Come DOWN"—the "come" of ACCEPTANCE.

In Matthew 11:28 is "Come UNTO"—the "come" of SATISFACTION.

In II Corinthians 6:17 is "Come OUT"—the "come" of SEPARATION.

In Luke 9:23 is "Come AFTER"—the "come" of DISCIPLESHIP.

In Song of Solomon 4:8 is "Come WITH"—the "come" of FELLOWSHIP.

In Revelation 4:1 is "Come UP"—the "come" of RAPTURE.

He is saying to us in these days, "Come with *Me.*" Whatever the experience, however severe the test, or great the sorrow, we may be assured that we are with Him, and He with us in it and through it.

It is important to remember that just as numbers in the Bible have a real significance, so scriptural names mean something also. In recording the words of Scripture, the Holy Spirit chose names which have typical import. We see an example of that in verse 8. We are told that "Amana" means "covenant," reminding us that our relationship to Christ is based upon the sure foundation of the "everlasting covenant" between God the Father, and God the Son. "Shenir" means "glistening," indicating the glorious nature of our fellowship. "Hermon" means "lofty." So these three words tell us that when our Lord asks us to come with Him, it is to be a relationship and fellowship *sure, glorious,* and *high.* It is the attraction of such a Person and such communion which shall save us from the dangers of "lions' dens, and the mountains of the leopards."

J. 4:9—"Thou hast ravished my heart, my sister."

C. I. Scofield, in commenting upon this phrase, says, "The word 'sister' here is of infinitely delicate significance, intimating the very whiteness of purity in the midst of an ardour which is, like the shekinah, aglow but unspeakably holy. Sin has almost deprived us of the capacity even to stand with unshod feet before this burning bush."

The practical truth we learn here is that God regards the marriage relation as an infinitely holy one. As we are told in Hebrews 13:4, "Marriage is honourable in all, and the bed undefiled." Let no ascetic, Christian or not, dare to say otherwise! Much harm has been done by well-meaning, but mistaken, brethren and sisters who have presumed to improve upon God's standards, and would impose bondage upon the saints in matters in which our God intends us to enjoy liberty. Unquestionably many unhappy homes among Christian people have resulted from attempting to follow the advice and prohibitions of such writers. A holy marriage and a happy marriage relationship are not incompatible, but affinities.

K. 4:10—". . . how much better is thy love than wine."

In chapter 1, verse 2, we heard the Bride saying this very thing to the Bridegroom. And now he uses her own words to assure her that she is as precious to him as he is to her.

What abundant grace is ours, as we realize that we are dear to the Lord Jesus. And when we spend time in worship, pouring out to Him the overflow of adoring hearts, it seems as if He stores up the expressions of our devotion, and our hearts hear Him say the same to us. This is "joy unspeakable and full of glory."

L. 4:11—". . . the smell of thy garments is like the smell of Lebanon."

"Garments" in Scripture suggest testimony before others, the outward activities and attitudes by which other people judge the reality of our Christian profession. In Psalm 45:8 the Psalmist, writing prophetically of the Coming One, the Lord Jesus Christ, says, "All thy garments smell of myrrh, and aloes, and cassia, out of the ivory palaces . . ." Everywhere He went, His garments were fragrant—He reminded people of heaven. He desires that this may be true of us.

Dr. William L. Pettingill, beloved Bible teacher, tells the story of a friend of his who owns a clothing store in Wilmington, Delaware. One day a certain customer came in to purchase a suit, and the proprietor could tell from his manner of dress that he was from the rural districts. He asked him to remove his coat so that he might determine the size required. As he took off his garment, the store owner quickly said, "I know where you are from." "That's strange," said the man. "You have never seen me before, and this is the first time I have been in your store." "That's true, but I can tell you several things about your home. You live in the country." "Yes." "About six miles south, and four miles east of ———." "That's right." "You have a wood-burning stove in your kitchen, and when you take off your coat at home, you hang it upon a hook behind the stove." "Sure enough." "And you burn a special kind of oak wood in that stove; isn't that right?" "It certainly is." "Well, your garments betrayed you, for I came from that section of the country myself, and there isn't any smoke in the world that smells like the smoke from those oak logs."

How do our garments smell? Fragrant, reminding others of Christ? Or do they manifest the offensive odors of worldliness and hypocrisy?

M. 4:12-16—"A garden inclosed is my sister, my spouse; a spring shut up, a fountain sealed.

Thy plants are an orchard of pomegranates, with pleasant fruits; camphire, with spikenard,

Spikenard and saffron; calamus and cinnamon, with all trees of frankincense; myrrh and aloes, with all the chief of spices:

A fountain of gardens, a well of living waters, and streams from Lebanon.

Awake, O north wind; and come, thou south; blow upon my garden, that the spices thereof may flow out . . ."

The heavenly Gardener is the only One who could produce fruit and fragrance in these hearts and lives of ours. This garden is a productive garden because He has planted it. He said, "I have chosen you, and ordained you . . . that ye *should* bear fruit" (John 15:16).

The Bridegroom has said in verse 12 that his Bride is a "garden inclosed" (shut up), and so she calls upon the north wind, and the south, to blow upon her garden, that the spices thereof may *flow out.*

"Wind" in the Scriptures is one of the beautiful symbols used of the Holy Spirit. We recall, in Acts 2, in the record of the day of Pentecost, that while the disciples were gathered together in the upper room, to await the coming of the Holy Spirit, ". . . suddenly there came a sound from heaven as of a rushing mighty wind, and it filled all the house where they were sitting."

First, the Bride calls upon the north wind. The north wind, with its chilling blasts, is not always welcome. But we are told that the wind from the north is one of the most purifying factors in our lives, for it destroys many harmful and deadly germs, thus protecting human, animal, and vegetable life. We could not get along without it.

The north wind is purifying in our Christian lives, too, for sometimes it blows through our homes and blows certain things right out the window. We have seen the north wind of the Holy Spirit's power blow through and take certain books from the bookshelves in Christian homes, and certain music off the piano. Ah, yes, 'tis a purifying wind.

The north wind of God's providence blows across our lives.

He sends the winds of adversity to make us grow.

He sends the winds of testing to try our faith.

He sends the winds of affliction, that we really may come to know Him as the Burden-Bearer.

He sends the winds of disappointment, that we may learn to trust Him.

He sends the winds of changed plans, that we may learn to let Him make our plans.

He sends the winds of chastening, that we may become more like the Lord Jesus.

Thank God for the north wind!

But the Bride calls for the south wind also. The south wind, with its warmth, usually comes in times of spiritual meditation. Of course, if we do not take much time alone with the Lord, and with His written Word, we do not know a great deal about the south wind. But it is a very precious wind. The moments spent alone with Him bring the south wind. Then it is that we really find Him to be all that He longs to be to us. Then it is that we find Him to be a living, loving Person, not merely an historical figure about whom we read and hear sermons. He becomes real to us.

Then there is the south wind of God's providence also. Sometimes it blows across our lives and takes us to some Bible conference, or meeting of spiritual fellowship, where we are lifted upon the mountain-tops of blessing. Sometimes it sends to our homes some radiant Christian who seems to fairly radiate Christ, and we see, through that one, possibilities of Christlikeness we had not realized before. Sometimes the south wind blows a book into our hands, which furnishes just the food we need at a time when some special spiritual message is necessary.

We need both these winds, for the Lord does not use gardens or fountains from which there is no outflowing. He wants to use us as channels of blessing, that others may see Christ in and through us.

III. WHAT THE BRIDE SAYS ABOUT HERSELF

1. *THE DECLARATION*

A. 4:6—"Until the day break, and the shadows flee away, I will get me to the mountain of myrrh, and to the hill of frankincense."

2. *THE TYPICAL IMPLICATION*

Some have attributed the statement in verse 6 to the Bridegroom, but we are convinced that they are the words of the Bride. In verse 17 of chapter 2, she uses similar words, urging her Beloved to "turn . . . and be like a roe or a young hart upon the mountains of Bether." In verse 6 of chapter 4, she assures him that in "the waiting time" she will enjoy communion with him upon the heights of fragrance and blessing.

Surely here we have a typical suggestion of our Lord's purpose for us while we walk "through the valley of the shadow of death" (Psa. 23:4). The Psalmist's primary reference certainly is to this world as "the valley of the shadow," not to death itself. There is coming a time of "daybreak," when the shadows shall flee away. Millions of believers throughout the ages have passed through the experience of physical death. Perhaps multitudes more shall thus enter the presence of the Lord. But one day our Lord shall come again, and multitudes living shall not see death, but shall be "changed," given their glorified bodies, and "caught up to meet the Lord in the air."

Some speak of death as the "sunset." Not so. For the Christian it is "daybreak"—it is sunrise. One has said, "Christ has made of death a narrow, starlit strip, between associations of yesterday and the reunions of tomorrow." Death is still "an enemy" (I Cor. 15:26), but it is a defeated enemy, and Christ has removed the "sting" from it.

The "myrrh" speaks of anointing, and the word "mountain" occurring here, signifying strength or power, suggests to us that while walking "through the valley of the shadow," it is our privilege to have the Holy Spirit's anointing for power in service and testimony.

The "frankincense" suggests the fragrance of a holy life and walk, the provision for which is completely available to us in Christ.

3. *THE NEW TESTAMENT REVELATION*

A. I Corinthians 15:55-58—"O death, where is thy sting? O grave, where is thy victory?
The sting of death is sin: and the strength of sin is the law.

But thanks be to God, which giveth us the victory through our Lord Jesus Christ.

Therefore, my beloved brethren, be ye steadfast, unmoveable, always abounding in the work of the Lord, forasmuch as ye know that your labour is not in vain in the Lord."

Colossians 3:2, 4—"Set your affection on things above, not on things on the earth . . .

When Christ, who is our life, shall appear, then shall ye also appear with him in glory."

4. *THE PRACTICAL APPLICATION*

A. 4:6—"Until the day break, and the shadows flee away, I will get me to the mountains of myrrh, and to the hill of frankincense."

Someone has said, "Learn to hold loosely all that is not eternal." And another puts the same truth this way, "Serve the Lord, and walk the paths of Christian experience *with Eternity's values in view.*"

That is the main practical lesson of this verse. The Bride realizes that there is to be a "daybreak," a time when "the shadows shall flee away," and until that time, she desires to walk as one possessed of the fragrance of her Beloved.

May this be true of us! May every word, every thought, every act, every ambition, be motivated by the prospect of seeing our Lord face to face at "daybreak." The judgment of the believer's *sins* is past. That took place at Calvary in the Person of our Substitute, the Lord Jesus. But there is coming the judgment seat of Christ (I Cor. 3:11-17) where our works, as Christians, shall be judged, and where there shall be "rewards" or "loss," according to the result of the review of them which shall take place there. This is a solemnizing thought. May the Holy Spirit make the reality of it a tremendous force for good in every department of our lives and service.

IV. WHAT THE BRIDEGROOM SAYS ABOUT HIMSELF

1. *THE DECLARATION*

A. 5:1—"I am come into my garden, my sister, my spouse: I have gathered my myrrh with my spice; I have eaten my honeycomb with my honey; I have drunk my wine with my milk: eat, O friends; drink, yea, drink abundantly, O beloved."

2. *THE TYPICAL IMPLICATION*

This statement of the Bridegroom, in response to the Bride's invitation in the last sentence of verse 16 of chapter 4, furnishes a beautiful illustration of Christ, in a threefold reference to the individual believer.

First, He calls the believer "My garden." That is His POSSESSION of the believer (John 17:10).

Second, He gathers fruit from the believer's service. That is FRUITFULNESS through the believer (John 15:5).

Third, He invites others to Himself through the believer. That is the WITNESS of the Holy Spirit in the believer (John 14:16, 17).

3. *THE NEW TESTAMENT REVELATION*

A. Galatians 2:20—"I am crucified with Christ: nevertheless I live; yet not I, but Christ liveth in me: and the life which I now live in the flesh I live by the faith of the Son of God, who loved me, and gave himself for me."

Revelation 3:20—"Behold, I stand at the door, and knock: if any man hear my voice, and open the door, I will come in to him, and will sup with him, and he with me."

Revelation 22:17—"And the Spirit and the bride say, Come. And let him that heareth say, Come. And let him that is athirst come. And whosoever will, let him take the water of life freely."

4. *THE PRACTICAL APPLICATION*

A. 5:1—"I am come into my garden, my sister, my spouse: I have gathered my myrrh with my spice; I have eaten my honeycomb with my honey; I have drunk my wine with my milk: eat, O friends; drink, yea, drink abundantly, O beloved."

There is a wealth of precious practical instruction in this verse. How wonderful that our Lord thinks of us as His garden, with all that figure involves of fragrance, fertility, freshness, and fruitfulness. And because He is the Gardener, ours is truly a "Victory garden." May we never fail Him in all that He looks for in His garden!

Did you notice the four phrases of three words each in this verse? "I am come,"—"I have gathered,"—"I have eaten,"—"I have drunk."

"I am come"; He did not wait for *us* to come to *Him*. We recall that "the Son of man *is come* to seek and to save that which was lost" (Luke 19:10). He said, "I am *come* that they might have life, and that they might have it more abundantly" (John 10:10). He was willing to come, and still He is eager to come into His garden, to enjoy the fragrance of the open heart of His own.

"I have gathered"; "myrrh" in Scripture sometimes seems to symbolize sorrow and tears. Which reminds us that our Lord is afflicted in all our afflictions (Isa. 63:9). Nothing touches us without touching Him first. He gathers—takes account of—these experiences of special sorrow and testing, and so weaves the design that they "all . . . work together for good" (Rom. 8:28) and for His glory. There is a "needs be" for every trial of our faith (I Pet. 1:6), and it is precious in His sight. He delights to "gather myrrh" in His garden.

"I have eaten"; honey is a symbol of sweetness. Our

Heavenly Gardener finds His garden sweet to His taste. Can it be? Yes, for He is the One who has *given* to us the sweetness of Himself. The Apostle, in II Corinthians 2:14, has said, ". . . we are unto God a sweet savour of Christ."

"I have drunk"; "wine" is a scriptural symbol of joy, and we learn that our Lord Jesus finds joy in us who belong to Him. "These things have I spoken unto you," said He, "that my joy might remain in you, and that your joy might be full" (John 15:11). "Milk" suggests food for the newborn babe, and when we hear, as it were, our Lord saying, "I have drunk my wine with my milk," we are comforted in the realization that He cares for all in His garden, the mature believer, who has reached the place of spiritual ripeness and experience characterized by strength and vigor; but He also includes in His tender concern the babe in Christ, still in the stage of sweet simplicity, growing and developing in grace and knowledge. The story is told of an antagonistic unbeliever who, aggravated by the simple faith of a little child who was rejoicing in the lovely prospect of being with Jesus forever, asked her, "But what if Jesus were in hell?" "Oh," replied the child, "but it would not be hell if He were there." Beautiful faith, and how satisfying an answer. Our Lord surely drinks deeply of such "milk."

How amazing is the thought that we may give satisfaction to the Lord Jesus. So often we speak of "being satisfied with Him," but is He satisfied with us? As He walks through the garden of our lives, does He find true satisfaction?

The Bridegroom does not enjoy the garden all by himself, but summons others to enjoy it with him. We have the privilege of being the gardens through whom others may find Christ real and satisfying. Spurgeon tells how they used to perfume the wings of doves, that other doves might be attracted to the dovecote.

"Did someone see Christ in you today? O Christian,
Look to your life, I pray;
The little things you've done and said . . .
Did they accord with the way you prayed?
Have your thoughts been pure, your words been kind,
Have you sought to have the Saviour's mind?
The world with its criticizing view . . .
Has watched, Did it see Christ in you?

"Did someone see Christ in you today? O Christian,
Look to your heart, I pray;
Has it led you near to the Father's throne,
Far away from the tempting one?
Have your feet on errands of love been sent,
Or with selfish deeds your life been spent?
Has some wandering soul with hope born new
Found Christ through following after you?

"Did someone see Christ in you today? O Christian,
Look to your light, I pray;
There are aching hearts and blighted souls
Being lost on sin's destructive shoals,
And perhaps of Christ, their only view
Is what of Him they see in you.
Have they seen enough of hope and cheer,
Look to your light, does it shine out clear?

"Did someone see Christ in you today? O Christian,
Be careful, watch and pray;
Look up to Christ in faith, and then
Lift up to Him your fellow men.
Upon your own strength you cannot rely,
There's a fountain of grace and strength on high,
Look up to that Fount for strength anew,
And the life of Christ will shine through you."

Section Four

SONG OF SOLOMON 5:2-5:5

I. WHAT THE BRIDE SAYS ABOUT THE BRIDE-GROOM

1. *THE DECLARATION*

A. 5:2—"... the voice of my beloved that knocketh."

B. 5:4—"My beloved put in his hand by the hole of the door . . ."

2. *THE TYPICAL IMPLICATION*

The typical implication of this section is beautiful, but solemn. It is the picture of the Lord Jesus standing outside the innermost heart of the believer, and appealing to that believer by the "knock" and the "voice." The believer has fallen into a state of spiritual sleepiness and lethargy, *immediately following a time of highest spiritual blessing.* We shall have more to say about this when we consider the practical features of the portion.

Dr. H. A. Ironside, in his excellent book, "Addresses on the Song of Solomon," gives us an important picture of Oriental custom, suggested by verse 4: "We will not understand the simile (in verse 4) unless we are familiar with those eastern doors and locks. The lock was on the inside of the door, and there was an opening where the owner could, if he had the key, reach in and use the key from the inside to open the door. He comes, but he does not open the door in that way. He has asked admission and wants the Bride to arise and open for him. She sees that hand come through the opening and the moment she does so, her heart is stirred and she cries, 'Oh, I must let him in.' And now she arises and hurries to the door and even as she lays hold of the lock, she exclaims, 'My hands dropped with myrrh, and my fingers with sweet-smelling myrrh, upon the handles of the lock.' That refers to another eastern custom. When a lover came to visit the one who had won his heart, and found that she was not at home, or if at home, she did not respond to his advances, he covered the lock of the door with sweet-smelling ointments and left flowers as a token of his affection. And so the Bride says, 'My hands dropped with myrrh.' It was not a dream then; he had really been there and had gone. But she threw the door open to enable him to hear her cry, 'Come, come in!' but there was no answering response. 'My beloved,' she said, 'had withdrawn himself and was gone.' "

3. *THE NEW TESTAMENT REVELATION*

A. Revelation 3:20—"Behold, I stand at the door, and knock: if any man hear my voice, and open the door, I will come in to him, and will sup with him, and he with me."

B. John 14:23, 24—"Jesus answered and said unto him, If a man love me, he will keep my words: and my Father will love him, and we will come unto him, and make our abode with him.

He that loveth me not keepeth not my sayings . . ."

4. *THE PRACTICAL APPLICATION*

A. 5:2—". . . the voice of my beloved that knocketh."

B. 5:4—"My beloved put in his hand by the hole of the door . . ."

In Section Three we have had a scene of sweet communion, in which there were evidences of fellowship and fruitfulness. It is a picture of the highest spiritual enjoyment. And then, immediately, there follows the note of separation, as seen in Section Four.

How often it is true that our times of spiritual laxness and coldness in Christian experience follow the periods of the keenest spiritual enjoyment. We are so human, so apt to become careless and reactionary, that we easily and quickly go from one extreme to the other.

We must consider, too, that Satan is most active toward us when we are enjoying the closest communion with Christ, and does all within his power to rob us of the ground gained, and to cancel the value of our spiritual progress. An old saint once said, "I need to pray more immediately following a spiritual victory than after a spiritual defeat."

These statements of the Bride concerning the Bridegroom so distinctly remind us of the words of the risen Chirst in Revelation 3:20, "Behold, I stand at the door, and knock: if any man hear my voice, and open the door, I will come in to him, and will sup with him, and he with me."

This verse in Revelation is a most familiar one, but like other familiar portions of Scripture, it is easy to read it casually and carelessly, and thus overlook some of the gems of truth hidden away under the surface.

Our Lord, in this verse, did *not* say, "If any man hear my *knock,*" but "my *voice.*" Think for a moment of that distinction—"I stand and *knock*"; "if any man hear my *voice.*"

The *knock* is given that we might hear His *voice*. The *knock* may be given in many ways. It must be something that arrests attention.

In the first place, it may come by *the Word of God, the Bible.* We may hear the knock through some great scriptural declaration, such as the claims of a holy God upon His creatures; or the great warnings concerning hell; or the revelations concerning the glories of heaven; or the majestic statements of the gospel of the grace of God.

The Lord *knocks* through His written Word.

And He *knocks* thus that we may hear His *voice.*

A missionary in India tells of a Brahman priest, an intelligent and open-minded man, who listened attentively to the preaching. He was given a Telugu Testament on condition that he would faithfully read it. He read it for a month; then, meeting the missionary again, he said in his native language, "I wish you to take the Book back. As I read it, it kicks me." He had heard the *knock.*

A touching story is told of an old chief in the New Hebrides who was watching Dr. Paton one day at work on the printing of the New Testament in the Ariwan language. "Does it speak?" inquired the old man, referring to the Book. "Yes," said Paton, "it can talk now in your own language." "Let it speak to me," said the man, "let me hear it speak." Paton read a few lines. "It does speak," cried the man. "Oh, give it to me!" He grasped the Book, turned it over and over, and cried in pleasure, "Make it speak to me again." He had heard the *knock.*

In the second place, the *knock* may come *through a sudden sorrow,* when a loved one is taken almost in an instant, leaving an aching void that only He, our blessed Lord, can fill. How many have heard the *knock* in the experience of bereavement. And as the Lord *knocks* thus, it is that we may hear His *voice* saying, "Blessed be God, even the Father of our Lord Jesus Christ, the father of mercies and the God of all comfort; who comforteth us in all our tribulation, that we may be able to comfort them which are in any trouble, by the comfort wherewith we ourselves are comforted of God" (II Cor. 1:3, 4).

"Coal tar is unsightly, nasty and messy, yet in the hands

of the chemists it becomes one of the most useful raw materials in the world. An eminent professor says, 'It is one of the strategic points in war and commerce. It wounds and heals. It supplies munitions and medicines. It is like a magic pursem from which anything can be drawn. The chemist puts his hand into the black mass and draws out all colors of the rainbow. This evil-smelling substance beats the rose in the production of perfume, and surpasses the honey-comb in sweetness.' Suffering and sorrow are never attractive. We do not want them to come into our lives, but if they do, they are the raw materials, like coal-tar, the products of which may help or hinder. We ourselves are the chemists. Out of the sorrow we may bring gentleness of spirit instead of bitterness; hope and not despair; patience and not cynicism."

"Speechless sorrow sat with me;
I was sighing wearily;
Lamp and fire were out; the rain
Wildly beat the window-pane;
In the dark we heard a knock,
And a hand was on the lock;
One in waiting spake to me
    Saying sweetly,
'I am come to sup with thee.'

"All my room was dark and damp;
'Sorrow,' said I, 'trim the lamp,
Light the fire, and cheer thy face,
Set the guest-chair in its place.'
And again I heard the knock,
In the dark I found the lock—
'Enter, I have turned the key—
    Enter, stranger,
Who art come to sup with me.'

"Opening wide the door, he came,
But I could not speak his name;
In the guest-chair took his place,
But I could not see his face,
When my cheerful fire was beaming,
When my little lamp was gleaming,
And the feast was spread for three,
Lo, my Master
Was the Guest that supped with me!"

Again, sometimes the *knock* comes *through sickness and physical affliction.* Have you ever thought that some of the experiences which the world calls "tragedies" and "calamities" are the most blessed of all possible experiences to the one whose ear is tuned to hear the *voice* of the Lord Jesus? How many Christians can testify that it was through the *knock* in time of illness that His precious *voice* was heard. As our Lord *knocks* thus, it is that we may hear His *voice* saying, "My grace is sufficient for thee."

Fourthly, sometimes the knock comes when *a great national emergency*—like a world war—separates members of families, completely alters plans for business, school, marriage, and other important phases of life. And as the Lord *knocks* thus, it is that we might hear His *voice* saying, "It is I, be not afraid. I will never leave thee, nor forsake thee."

In Oriental lands, it is customary for the visitor to knock at the door, and then the occupant of the house asks, "Who?" and hearkens for the response of the voice outside the door, "I." In the 12th chapter of Acts, after Peter was imprisoned, and was delivered miraculously in response to the prayers of the church, he came to the house of Mary, where many were gathered together in prayer for him. He knocked at the door, and we read (v.13) that a damsel named Rhoda "came to hearken." When she "knew Peter's *voice*" she ran to tell the others that Peter was there. She heard the *knock,* but it was Peter's *voice* that brought gladness.

The *unbeliever* can hear the *knockings* of the Lord, but only the one who knows Christ can truly hear His *voice.*

In the 22nd chapter of Acts is the record of Paul's defense before the multitude. He is telling the story of his conversion on the Damascus road, when a great light from heaven shone around about him and those with him. Paul said, "And they that were with me saw the light, and were afraid; but *they heard not the voice* of him that spake to me" (Acts 22:9).

When we hear His *voice,* and realize that it is the Lord of Glory seeking to come into our hearts and lives to have fellowship with us, how wonderful it is!

It is an individual matter, too. Each one must open the door, and say to the Lord Jesus, "Come in." There is no latch on the outside of the door. Our Lord will not force Himself upon us. He is waiting for us to open and let Him in.

This is more than *hearing about* the Lord.
This is more than *talking about* the Lord.
This is more than *reading about* the Lord.
It is personal communion with, and enjoyment of, Him.

When we open, and He truly comes in, He is the answer to every need, the remedy for every sin—He is complete satisfaction.

"Lord Jesus, I have found in Thee
Abundant *life;*
Life that as a river floweth,
Life that deeper, fuller groweth
'Mid earth's strife.

"Lord Jesus, I have found in Thee
Eternal *peace;*
Peace that passeth understanding,
Peace which, day by day expanding,
Shall not cease.

"Lord Jesus, I have found in Thee
Exceeding *joy;*
In Thy presence joy forever,
Joy which even Satan never
Can destroy.

"Lord Jesus, I have found in Thee
The *love* of God;
Perfect love that never faileth,
Love which evermore availeth
By Thy blood."

II. WHAT THE BRIDEGROOM SAYS ABOUT THE BRIDE

1. *THE DECLARATION*

A. 5:2—". . . my sister, my love, my dove, my undefiled."

2. *THE TYPICAL IMPLICATION*

Again we have a list of gracious epithets employed by the Bridegroom, to describe his affection for his loved one.

There are four words, "sister"—"love"—"dove"—"undefiled"—and each one prefaced by the personal pronoun "my."

Can anyone fail to see here the overflow of love, grace, and mercy, from the heart of Christ, for those whom He has purchased with His own precious blood?

Again we are reminded here that, even though we still are in the body, with "the flesh"—the old, sinful nature—still in us, "warring against the (Holy) Spirit" (Gal. 5:16, 17), our blessed Lord, whose vision is not restricted and limited by time, looks upon us, even now, as *positionally* perfect and complete, and rejoices in us as we shall be, actually, "some time soon." How can we restrain our hearts and lips from shouting, "Hallelujah!"

3. *THE NEW TESTAMENT REVELATION*

A. Galatians 3:26—"For ye are all the children of God by (through) faith in Christ Jesus."

Ephesians 3:17-19—"That Christ may dwell in your hearts by faith; that ye, being rooted and grounded in love,

May be able to comprehend with all saints what is the breadth, and length, and depth, and height; And to know the love of Christ, which passeth knowledge, that ye might be filled with all the fulness of God."

II Timothy 2:24—"And the servant of the Lord must not strive; but be gentle unto all men . . ." Matthew 5:48—"Be ye therefore perfect, even as your Father which is in heaven is perfect."

4. *THE PRACTICAL APPLICATION*

A. 5:2—". . . my sister, my love, my dove, my undefiled."

As we see this scene applied to Christ and the believer, we are impressed at once with the fact that these words are addressed to the object of His love, at the time there is a separation between them. Something has come in to interrupt the deep enjoyment of communion seen in Section Three. And yet, with Himself, outside the door, pleading with His loved one to admit Him, He uses these four words of lovely descriptiveness, "my sister"—"my love"—"my dove"—"my undefiled." Thus we remind ourselves that the *relationship* between Christ and the true believer is never broken, although the *fellowship* may be.

How rich are the names He uses for His own:
"My sister"—the name of *pure relationship*
"My love"—the name of *salvation* (John 3:16)
"My dove"—the name of *Christ-likeness*
"My undefiled"—the name of *wondrous grace.*

It is important to notice here that the Lord has not changed, even though the believer has. The love of Christ never changes toward His loved ones. He is "the same yesterday, and today, and forever" (Heb. 13:8). His love is not conditioned upon our attitudes and actions, but upon His eternal and unchangeable purposes. But how great is *our loss* when we miss, for even a brief moment, the sense of His presence and His smile.

This is the first time that the Bridegroom has called his Bride "my undefiled," and it is all the more remarkable that he uses the title, not while they are enjoying the closest fellowship, but at a time of separation. Could there possibly be a more tender appeal to the heart of the backsliding Christian than this gracious attitude on the part of our Saviour? We recall that when Peter denied his Lord, and spent those hours in the soul darkness of broken fellowship, it was a tender look from the Lord Jesus which brought him to the place of confession and repentance (Luke 22:61, 62).

III. WHAT THE BRIDE SAYS ABOUT HERSELF

1. *THE DECLARATION*

A. 5:2—"I sleep, but my heart waketh."

B. 5:3—"I have put off my coat; how shall I put it on? I have washed my feet; how shall I defile them?"

C. 5:5—"I rose up to open to my beloved; and my hands dropped with myrrh, and my fingers with sweet-smelling myrrh, upon the handles of the lock."

2. *THE TYPICAL IMPLICATION*

The picture suggested by this portion is that of a believer who, at first being in a lukewarm state, a half-and-half experience, is neither wide awake nor sound asleep. A part of him is awake—his heart—but "the flesh is weak," and he lacks the spiritual energy to put into practice that which he knows to be right, and according to the clear teaching of the Word of God. What a pathetic condition of soul, and yet how apt we are to find ourselves there. There are many steps in that direction—prayerlessness; failure to read, study, and meditate upon the Word; lack of courage and faithfulness in personal witnessing; a critical spirit; these, and many others, lead in the direction of spiritual lukewarmness.

But in the meantime the Beloved comes, and speaks, asking admittance, and there is the response, for she "rose up," and is now awake. Still there is yet much to be done before there can be thorough restoration of fellowship.

3. *THE NEW TESTAMENT REVELATION*

A. Revelation 3:15—"I know thy works, that thou art neither cold nor hot: I would thou wert cold or hot."

B. Romans 12:11—"Not slothful in business; fervent in spirit; serving the Lord."

C. Romans 6:13—"Neither yield ye your members as instruments of unrighteousness unto sin: but yield yourselves unto God, as those that are alive from the dead, and your members as instruments of righteousness unto God."

4. *THE PRACTICAL APPLICATION*

A. 5:2—"I sleep, but my heart waketh."

B. 5:3—"I have put off my coat; how shall I put it on? I have washed my feet; how shall I defile them?"

The picture here is of the believer who has deliberately left the place of close fellowship with Christ. The result is a condition of restlessness. There is neither the enjoyment of full wakefulness, nor the comfort of complete rest. The heart is wakeful, and cannot have real rest and peace without the conscious presence of the Lord Jesus.

There seems to be a bit of the impetuous in verse 3, for the word in the original language of the passage, translated "put off" means literally "stripped off," as if some force and haste were used, and some self-assertiveness and self-sufficience were in evidence. These hearts of ours are "deceitful above all things and desperately wicked." They need a Keeper, One who alone can understand and control them. The word "coat" is literally "tunic," which was the outer garment, and which is a symbol of practical righteousness—that which is seen by others as an indication of the reality of our Christian profession. One of the first results of a break in close fellowship with our Lord, is that our walk before others becomes less exemplary, and our steps are prone to wander from the scripturally prescribed paths.

The Bride seems to realize that she has been walking where she should not, for she says, "I have washed my feet." But she declares that *she* has done the washing. In John 13, where the Lord is seen washing the feet of His disciples, He said, "If *I* wash thee not, thou hast no part with me" (v.8). When we contact sin and defilement in our walk through this dark world, and so lose for a time the clear vision of His face, and the sweet sound of His voice, *we* cannot wash our feet and cleanse them, but we can submit our case to Him, and let Him do the cleansing, for "He is faithful and just to forgive us our sins, and to cleanse us from all unrighteousness" (I John 1:9).

One of the Satanic snares into which believers, as well as unbelievers, are apt to fall, when they are made conscious of their sin and need for cleansing, is the false idea that some ceremony, or ritual, or religious observance and activity, will serve to satisfy God and remove the barrier to our access to Him. Let us not be deceived. Christ is the Way. It is Christ—nothing more; nothing less; nothing else! *Let* Him!

> C. 5:5—"I rose up to open to my beloved; and my hands dropped with myrrh, and my fingers with sweet-smelling myrrh, upon the handles of the lock."

It is sadly possible for the believer to be out of fellowship with Christ—with our Lord outside the *bolted* door of the heart—and yet have his hands occupied with bits of "Christian service." Here the Bride's hands were "dropping myrrh," and the Bridegroom was outside a bolted door.

So many times we are apt to put service first, when, in our Lord's estimate, it is secondary, and communion with Himself assuming primary importance. In Mark 3:14 it is recorded that "He ordained twelve, *that they should be with him,* and that he might send them forth to preach." First, companionship with Himself, then service. God always honors His Word, His gospel, when it is preached. But there is a solemn thought in the possibility of a believer being most active with good things, and yet with a heart not resting in perfect enjoyment of the Person of the Lord Jesus. It is thoroughly scriptural to use the slogan, "To know Him, and to make Him known." First, Himself; then sharing Him with others.

The "in and out" of John 10:9 is the divine principle. First, *"in"* for fellowship; then *"out"* for service. Not "out" first to serve; then "in" to ask His blessing upon the bit of service. That will not do. That is not God's way.

Is not the reason why Christian service becomes a drudge and a dull procedure at times, that in personal witnessing, in teaching the Sunday school class, in preaching, in leading the prayer meeting, in directing the missionary society, in singing in the choir, in the daily routine, we have been going "out" before we have gone "in"? We have been exactly reversing God's order.

Someone has said, "A Christian worker is good; a worker in Christ is better; but Christ in a worker is best."

IV. WHAT THE BRIDEGROOM SAYS ABOUT HIMSELF

1. *THE DECLARATION*

A. 5:2—". . . my head is filled with dew, and my locks with the drops of the night."

2. *THE TYPICAL IMPLICATION*

Surely, in the reference to "the dew," and the larger "drops of the night" we have a twofold typical suggestion of Gethsemane and Calvary—that awful darkness through which the Son of God passed, that we might never have to endure that darkness. "For He hath made Him to be sin for us, who knew no sin; that we might be made the righteousness of God in Him" (II Cor. 5:21).

"Dew" also may be an illustration of the working of the Holy Spirit.

3. *THE NEW TESTAMENT REVELATION*

A. Luke 22:42-44—". . . Father, if thou be willing, remove this cup from me: nevertheless not my will, but thine, be done. And there appeared an angel unto him from heaven, strengthening him.

And being in an agony he prayed more earnestly; and his sweat was as it were great drops of blood falling down to the ground."

Matthew 27:46—". . . My God, My God, why hast forsaken me?"

John 16:7—"Nevertheless I tell you the truth; it is expedient for you that I go away: for if I go not away, the Comforter will not come unto you; but if I depart, I will send him unto you."

4. *THE PRACTICAL APPLICATION*

The references to "dew" and "drops of the night" (rain), in addition to the typical significance in connection with the suffering and death of our Lord, have a most practical bit of instruction for us.

We are reminded of the song of Moses, as contained in the 32nd chapter of Deuteronomy. In verses 1 to 4 we read, "Give ear, O ye heavens, and I will speak; and hear, O earth, the words of my mouth. My doctrine shall drop as the *rain,* my speech shall distil as the *dew,* as the *small rain* upon the tender herb, and as the *showers* upon the grass: Because I will publish the name of the Lord: ascribe ye greatness unto our God. He is the Rock, his work is perfect: for all his ways are judgment: a God of truth and without iniquity, just and right is he."

When Moses was to publish good news concerning the Lord, he knew that the results would be as dew, small rain,

rain, and showers upon a parched earth. So shall it be with us, as we publish "the gospel of the grace of God," and "preach Christ." Thirsty, dry, arid souls will be refreshed and become fruitful.

In the figure used of the "dew," there is also a lovely suggestion of the working of the Holy Spirit. The dew does not appear unless the circumstances be calm. It is not distilled when the atmosphere is disturbed or stormy. The Holy Spirit's work and power are realized and appropriated when the life of the believer is calm, unruffled, and yielded. The Holy Spirit finds His vehicle for effectual working in the heart free from anxiety, profitless rush, and fleshly energy. One writer has given us a beautiful word-picture of the poise and balance of our Lord in this analysis of His perfect character: "He was a critic but never a cynic. He was brave but not a hero. He was firm but not obstinate. He was pious but not impractical. He was humble but not cowardly. He was gentle but not effeminate. He was superior to the world but craved its sympathy. He was dignified but simple. He was cheerful but never humorous. He was temperate but not austere. His fortitude never became fatalism. His generosity never became indulgence. He was youthful in years but venerable as the ages in influence. He was keen but not impatient. His enthusiasm contained no fanaticism. He respected authority, but demanded that the world, from Caesar down, and the generations of the future, should yield Him allegiance. He never apoligized. He never said anything or did anything that needed an apology. He walked the earth like a King, but preserved the attitude of a servant. No mere earthly king could live as He lived and maintain his dignity. But He did, and continues to do so."

Truly our Lord can say, ". . . my head is filled with dew, and my locks with the drops of the night."

Section Five

SONG OF SOLOMON 5:6-6:3

I. WHAT THE BRIDE SAYS ABOUT THE BRIDEGROOM

1. *THE DECLARATION*

A. 5:6—". . . my beloved had withdrawn himself, and was gone."

B. 5:10-16—"My beloved is white and ruddy, the chiefest among ten thousand. His head is as the most fine gold, his locks are bushy, and black as a raven. His eyes are as the eyes of doves by the rivers of waters, washed with milk, and fitly set.

His cheeks are as a bed of spices, as sweet flowers: his lips like lilies, dropping sweet-smelling myrrh. His hands are as gold rings set with the beryl: his belly is as bright ivory overlaid with sapphires.

His legs are as pillars of marble, set upon sockets of fine gold: his countenance is as Lebanon, excellent as the cedars. His mouth is most sweet: yea, he is altogether lovely. This is my beloved, and this is my friend, O daughters of Jerusalem."

C. 6:2, 3—"My beloved is gone down into his garden, to the beds of spices, to feed in the gardens, and to gather lilies . . . he feedeth among the lilies."

2. *THE TYPICAL IMPLICATION*

In these two statements of the Bride concerning the Bridegroom, we see a twofold typical illustration.

First, in her declaration to the effect that her Beloved had withdrawn himself, and was gone, we see the danger of delay in opening the door to Christ, whatever be the reason for His knock. The *sinner,* not yet born again, but hearing the gentle knock of the Holy Spirit's convicting power, jeopardizes his eternal welfare by procrastination. The *saint,* hearing the call of the Lord Jesus to specific service, to separation, to communion—whatever the distinct "knock" may be—loses inestimably by delay in response. As the Bride, in verse 3, began to make excuses, thus causing delay in "rising to open," paid the penalty in the loss of his personal presence and companionship.

Second, in the Bride's ten-fold description of the Bridegroom, we see, of course, a marvelous typical representation of the risen, living Christ. As the "Daughters of Jerusalem" (professing Christendom) ask her (v. 9) in a challenging manner, about her Beloved, she is "ready always to give an answer" (I Pet. 3:15), and does so in a most complete and impassioned manner.

3. *THE NEW TESTAMENT REVELATION*

A. Ephesians 5:18-20—"And be not drunk with wine, wherein is excess; but be filled with the (Holy) Spirit; Speaking to yourselves in psalms and hymns and spiritual songs, singing and making melody in your heart to the Lord; Giving thanks always for all things unto God and the Father in the name of our Lord Jesus Christ." Revelations 1:12-18—"And I turned . . . and saw . . . in the midst of the seven candlesticks one like unto the Son of man, clothed with a garment

> down to the foot, and girt about the paps with a golden girdle. His head and his hairs were white like wool, as white as snow; and his eyes were as a flame of fire; And his feet like unto fine brass, as if they burned in a furnace; and his voice as the sound of many waters. And he had in his right hand seven stars: and out of his mouth went a sharp twoedged sword: and his countenance was as the sun shineth in his strength. And when I saw him, I fell at his feet as dead. And he laid his right hand upon me, saying unto me, Fear not; I am the first and the last: I am he that liveth, and was dead; and, behold, I am alive forevermore . . ."

4. *THE PRACTICAL APPLICATION*

Under "Typical Implication" we have sounded the warning against delay in response to the call of the Lord Jesus, whatever form that call may take. Ready, quick obedience means fruitfulness and blessing in the Christian life, with a continuous sense of the personal presence of the Lord. Dullness of hearing and delay in responding to His voice may mean loss of great blessing in the daily path here, and loss of reward at the judgment seat of Christ (I Cor. 3:11-15). How sad to see a young life, possessed with vigor, talent, and real promise—lying dormant and fruitless because there has been failure or willfull neglect in respect to the call of the Lord. He has "withdrawn himself, and is gone" so far as real use of that life is concerned.

How sad also, to see a life, once so greatly used in the service of Christ, now so empty and fruitless—all because sin, in some form, has come in to clog the channel of Holy Spirit blessing and power. "He has withdrawn himself, and is gone."

The law of atrophy applies to the sphere of Christian service and testimony—"Use, or lose." Dr. Griffith-Thomas used to say, "Christian service and growth are like riding a bicycle—either you keep going, or you fall off."

If these pages should fall into the hands of one who is conscious that, so far as his usefulness in Christian service and testimony is concerned, the Lord Jesus "has withdrawn himself, and is gone," because sin, carelessness, and indifference have crept in to mar the communion, will you not, right now, before you continue with the reading, come to Him, in humble confession (I John 1:9), claiming that forgiveness and cleansing which He promises to *you?* He longs to use you again, and bless you, and make you a blessing; and He will.

In verse 10, the Bride gives a *general* description of her Bridegroom, and then in verses 11 to 16, a detailed account of his features, and in verse 16, another general phrase of description, "Yea, he is altogether lovely."

In chapter 4, the Bridegroom gives *seven* features in describing the Bride, but here the Bride mentions *ten* in describing the Bridegroom. The number ten is made up of *seven,* the number of divine *completeness,* and *three,* the number of divine *perfection.* Both are seen in the Lord Jesus Christ, and in His eternal purposes in redemption.

"My beloved is white and ruddy." "White" describes the purity of the Person of Christ. And it also suggests the cleansing of the sinner who is made clean through the "washing of regeneration" (Titus 3:5). "Ruddy" reminds us of His precious shed blood, the sacrifice which, once for all, paid the debt for our sins (I Pet. 2:24). ". . . Unto him that loved us, and *washed* us from our sins in his own *blood"* (Rev. 1:5).

"His head is as the most fine gold." This may suggest two things as applied to the Lord Jesus. It may stand for

supreme rulership, as in the word to Nebuchadnezzar, "Thou art this head of gold" (Dan. 2:38). Also it may represent perfect righteousness in the Person of Christ (Rev. 1:13).

". . . his locks are bushy, and black as a raven." These adjectives, describing the hair, remind us of the youth, strength, and vitality of our Lord. It is well to remember that, while He has always been—He never began to be—"from everlasting to everlasting" He is God the Son—yet He did come *into the world* as man, and accomplished His blessed purposes here as a *young* man. He was "in the beginning . . . God" (John 1:1); "the Father of the ages" (Isa. 9:6), typified by the *white* hair mentioned in Revelation 1:13, yet He was only about thirty-three years of age, as we reckon time, when He went to Calvary. Isn't it precious to realize that He is now in Glory, as a *young man,* understanding the problems, and temptations, and joys of youth, as well as the burdens, and sorrows, and testings of old age?

"His eyes are as the eyes of doves by the rivers of waters, washed with milk, and fitly set." Those who die and pass into eternity without being "born again," without receiving the Lord Jesus Christ as Saviour, shall have to stand before the piercing, awful, fiery glance of those eyes at the judgment of the Great White Throne (Rev. 20:11-15). In Revelation 5:6 we have John's mention of "the Lamb" (Christ)—"And I beheld, and, lo, in the midst of the throne and of the four beasts, and in the midst of the elders, stood a Lamb as it had been slain, having seven horns and seven eyes, which are the seven Spirits of God sent forth into all the earth." This same Jesus, who came to be the Saviour, the Redeemer of men, shall one day be the Judge of those who have turned from God's gracious offer of the free gift of eternal life.

But to those who are members of Him, who have received Him who is our Life, His eyes now, and throughout eternity, are loving, and tender, and beautiful. He says to us, "I will guide thee with mine eye" (Psa. 32:8). We have no fear when those eyes look upon us, for we know that they are as "eyes of doves by the rivers of waters." They look upon us with the joy of blood-bought possessiveness, and we rejoice in His glance.

Of course, some of us may be in the backslidden condition of Peter, when he denied his Lord, and we, like Peter, may need to have the Lord Jesus look upon us in tender rebuke and loving reproof (Luke 22:63) that our hearts may be broken in confession and return to Him. If so, let us not delay. His eyes will look upon us in grace and mercy.

We shall find His eyes to be *"washed with milk"*—clear, seeing all—not a thing, however small, can escape His gaze. One recalls that, as a boy, his mother used to wash his eyes with warm milk, to relieve a granulated lid condition, and to clarify the vision which otherwise might be obstructed and cloudy. Our Lord always sees with perfect vision. Dear child of God, do not become depressed through the fear that the Lord has overlooked you, or regards your problems as too small for His concern. He sees, He knows, and, best of all, He has made complete and satisfactory provision, in Himself, for every one of your needs.

His eyes are *"fitly set,"* like a precious jewel in its setting, with all beauty and fitness.

"His cheeks are as a bed of spices, as sweet flowers." As we think of the cheeks of our Lord, our minds and hearts are taken back to the scene described prophetically in Isaiah 50:6, "I gave my back to the smiters, and my *cheeks* to them that plucked off the hair: I hid not my *face* from shame and spitting." That is the scene of grace, where He who had no sin *in* Him, took our sins *upon* Him, that we, believing upon Him, might have everlasting life.

But again we see the scene of *judgment* in Revelation 20:11, when this same Jesus shall sit upon the Judgment

Throne, "from whose *face* the earth and heaven fled away."

". . . His lips like lilies, dropping sweet smelling myrrh." We are reminded of the word in Psalm 45:2, written by the Psalmist in anticipation of the Christ to whose coming the Old Testament saints looked forward, ". . . grace is poured into thy lips." He calls now, today, this moment, in perfect grace, "Come unto me, all ye that labour and are heavy laden, and I will give you rest" (Matt. 11:28).

> "Majestic sweetness sits enthroned
> Upon the Saviour's brow;
> His head with radiant glories crowned,
> His *lips* with grace o'erflow."

"His hands are as gold rings set with beryl." What shall we say of those blessed hands? They are hands of *power* with which He created all things (Col. 1:16-18; John 1:3); they are the hands of *mercy,* with which He "went about doing good" (Acts 10:38); of *grace,* outstretched to the sinner (Matt. 11:28-30); of *strength,* with which He sustains His own (John 10:27-31); hands *nail-pierced,* as our *Substitute* (I Pet. 2:24); of *love* (Song of Solomon 2:6); of *beauty* (Song of Solomon 5:14).

An aged believer who had been going through a time of special testing through affliction, was visited by her young pastor, who desired to be helpful, but hadn't had the "seasoning" of experience in his own life. He said, "Well, Mother, remember that you are held in the hollow of the Lord's hands, and that you cannot slip through His fingers." "Oh," she replied, with a twinkle in her eye, "I am sure of that, for *I am one of His fingers."* Ah, yes, that dear soul had caught the blessed truth of identification—"we are members of his body, of his flesh, and of his bones" (Eph. 5:30). We are "graven upon the palms of His hands" (Isa. 49:16).

"His belly is as bright ivory overlaid with sapphires." This speaks of His tender compassion, ". . . his compassions

fail not" (Lam. 3:22). "His lovingkindness, Oh, how great."

Paul makes the practical application in Philippians 2:1, 2, "If there be therefore any consolation in Christ, if any comfort of love, if any fellowship of the Spirit, if any bowels (tender compassions) and mercies, Fulfil ye my joy, that ye be likeminded, having the same love, being of one accord, of one mind."

"His legs are as pillars of marble, set upon sockets of fine gold." This refers, typically, to the walk. We find a reference to its typical significance in Psalm 25:10, "All the *paths* of the Lord are mercy and truth unto such as keep his covenant and his testimonies." "Pillars of marble" denote strength, and "sockets of fine gold" suggest perfect righteousness. Could any other two words more perfectly describe the walk, the path, of our blessed Lord when He was here upon earth? And surely they shall be characteristic of His rule when He shall come again to reign in majestic strength and perfect righteousness. There will be no "political pull" in that Kingdom; no graft or bribery of that Ruler; no personal favorites. All will be perfect justice, equity and righteousness when the King of kings, and Lord of lords sits upon His throne.

". . . his countenance is as Lebanon, excellent as the cedars." This may be taken to refer to the general appearance of our Lord. "Cedar" is sweet and stately. In Revelation 1:16 we read, concerning the glorified Christ, ". . . his *countenance* was as the sun shineth in his strength." And the Psalmist prays (Psalm 4:6) "There be many that say, Who will shew us any good? Lord, lift thou up the light of thy *countenance* upon us." And again, in Psalm 42:5, "Why art thou cast down, O my soul? and why art thou disquieted in me? hope thou in God: for I shall yet praise him for the help of his *countenance."*

Then there is another promise concerning those who know the joyful sound of the gospel, ". . . they shall walk, O Lord, in the light of thy *countenan*[illegible]"

"His mouth is most sweet . . ." His *lips* have been referred to in verse 13, and we thought particularly of His grace as we considered them. Here, some have thought that a reference might be made to the *music* of His voice. How sweet is that voice as it comes to His own in the darkness of sad circumstance, and affliction, and disappointment. Just to know that "He is near, to comfort and cheer, just when we need Him most." Can any voice compare with His?

> Oh, I love to hear His voice,
> Saying, "You belong to Me;
> You are not your own,
> With a price you're bought,
> And you're Mine eternally."
>
> Oh, I love to hear Him say,
> "I have saved you by My grace";
> And when I get to glory
> It will then be grander still,
> For I shall see His face.

"Yea, he is altogether lovely. This is my beloved, and this is my friend, O daughters of Jerusalem." Now the Bride reaches the place where she has fairly exhausted words to describe her Beloved. And she just sums it all up by the words, "Yea, he is altogether lovely." "*My* beloved"; "*My* friend." Personal possession. Reality. Friendship.

An unknown author has given us the following remarkable statement concerning "the incomparable Christ."

"He became Son of Man that we might become sons of God. He came from Heaven, where winds never blow, flowers never fade. They never 'phone for a doctor, for there no one is ever sick. No undertakers and no graveyards for no one ever dies—no one is ever buried.

"He lived in poverty and was reared in obscurity. He had no wealth nor influence and had neither training nor education. His relatives were inconspicuous and uninfluential.

"In infancy He startled a king; in boyhood He puzzled the doctors; in manhood He walked upon the billows and hushed the sea to sleep. He healed the multitudes without medicine and made no charge for His services. He never wrote a book, yet not all the libraries of the country could hold all the books that could be written about Him. He never wrote a song, yet He has furnished the theme of more songs than all the song-writers combined. He never founded a college, yet all the schools together cannot boast of as many students as He has. Great men have come and gone, yet He lives on. Death could not destroy Him, the grave could not hold Him.

"He laid aside His purple robe for a peasant's gown. He was rich, yet for our sake He became poor. How poor? Ask Mary! Ask the Wise Men! He slept in another's manger. He cruised the lake in another's boat. He rode on another man's ass. He was buried in another man's tomb. All failed, but He never. The ever Perfect One, He is the Chief among ten thousand. He is altogether lovely."

In the third chapter of Romans, verses 13 to 18, we see the condition of the natural man, the unsaved man. There we have a picture of the awful, the sinful state of his *throat,* his *tongue,* his *lips,* his *mouth,* his *feet,* and his *eyes.* What a contrast is our picture, in the Song of Solomon, of our Beloved, the Lord Jesus, in which these various features are mentioned for eternal blessing, rather than for curse. And God's matchless grace has transformed *us,* who were under the curse of sin, but who are now in Christ. Praise His name forever!

In this section there are no statements by the Bridegroom concerning the Bride, for she is seeking him who is absent. So we come to division three:

III. WHAT THE BRIDE SAYS ABOUT HERSELF

1. *THE DECLARATION*

A. 5:6-8—". . . I opened to my beloved . . . my soul failed when he spake: I sought him, but I could not find him; I called him, but he gave me no answer. The watchmen that went about the city found me, they smote me, they wounded me; the keepers of the walls took away my veil from me. . . . I am sick of (with) love."

B. 6:3—"I am my beloved's, and my beloved is mine . . ."

2. *THE TYPICAL IMPLICATION*

The scene, as described in these few verses, is typically suggestive of the Christian who, out of fellowship with the Lord Jesus, is in ill favor and disrepute in three other directions, namely, with other true believers; with mere professing Christians; and with the world at large, which is openly at enmity against Christ. We see this thought suggested by "the watchmen," "the keepers of the walls," and "the daughters of Jerusalem."

In the story of Peter's denial of his Lord, as recorded in Luke 22, we see that Peter "followed afar off" (v.54). We see also that he was warming himself at the wrong fire (v.55), and was discovered by the enemies of the Lord to be in the wrong company (vv.56-60). When a child of God gets into worldly practices and company, the world itself will point the finger of scorn at him, as if to say, "You know better than this. You do not belong upon this level. You are acting beneath the standards which you claim for yourself."

When David sinned with Bathsheba, the word of the Lord, through Nathan, came to him, ". . . by this deed thou hast given great occasion to the enemies of the Lord to blaspheme" (II Sam. 12:14). When the believer sins, and thus interrupts communion between himself and his Lord, he furnishes an excuse to unsaved sinners to "sin without conscience," and to blaspheme.

In "the taking away of the veil" (5:7) the Bride was subjected to the greatest disgrace possible to the Oriental woman, for thus she was exposed to great indignity and reproach. She became, temporarily at least, like a "woman of the streets," without the protective badge of her station and rank. When, through sin, the true Christian, even for a brief time, steps down from the high calling to which the grace of God has elevated him, it is no great surprise if the enemies of God and merely nominal Christians "remove his veil," so to speak, and "catalogue" him as a pretender and a hypocrite.

3. *THE NEW TESTAMENT REVELATION*

A. Hebrews 11:6—"But without faith it is impossible to please him: for he that cometh to God must believe that he is, and that he is a rewarder of them that diligently seek him."

B. James 4:1-4—"From whence come wars and fightings among you? come they not hence, even of your lusts that war in your members? Ye lust, and have not: ye kill, and desire to have, and cannot obtain: ye fight and war, yet ye have not, because ye ask not. Ye ask, and receive not, because ye ask amiss, that ye may consume it upon your lusts. Ye adulterers and adulteresses, know ye not that the friendship of the world is enmity with God? whosoever therefore will be a friend of the world is the enemy of God."

C. Galatians 6:1, 2—"Brethren, if a man be overtaken in a fault, ye which are spiritual, restore such an one in the spirit of meekness; considering thyself, lest thou also be tempted. Bear ye one another's burdens, and so fulfil the law of Christ."

4. *THE PRACTICAL APPLICATION*

A. 5:6-8—". . . I opened to my beloved . . . my soul failed when he spake: I sought him, but I could

> not find him; I called him, but he gave me no answer. The watchmen that went about the city found me, they smote me, they wounded me; the keepers of the walls took away my veil from me. . . . I am sick of (with) love."

In verse 6 we are reminded practically that sin interferes with personal communion with our Lord, and also interferes with effectual prayer. How sad are the words, "I could not find him," and "he gave me no answer." How many of the saints of God are right at this point today! No victory, no power in testimony, no genuine enjoyment of the Person of the Lord Jesus, no joyous prayer ministry. Sin, the world, material things, selfish plans and ambitions, laziness, neglect of the reading and study of Scripture—these, and more, have crept into the life and robbed it of poise, balance, buoyancy, and joy.

The words of the Lord in John 15:7 still are true, "If ye abide in me, and my words abide in you, ye shall ask what ye will, and it shall be done unto you." Practical abiding in Christ consists in the believer recognizing all that he is in Christ positionally, and, in view of that fact, being wholly yielded to Christ—His word and His will—obedient, trustful, and completely surrendered.

Just a few words here as to scriptural "sanctification." There is much misunderstanding among the children of God as to this important subject. For example, some think of sanctification as being a process by means of which the Christian becomes better and better, until finally he reaches a state where he is "fit for heaven." But such is not the case at all. Everyone who, in simple faith, acknowledging himself to be a lost, helpless sinner, under the condemnation of God, with no ability in himself to meet God's holy demands, will receive the Lord Jesus Christ as Saviour, will receive eternal life the moment he believes in Him (John 3:16). To "receive eternal life" means to be eternally "in Christ" (Eph. 1), and to be "in Christ" means that we share His standing with the Father, and that we are as near to the Father as is He!

It is God's way to make the believer perfect in his *standing,* or *position,* before Him the moment he believes, and is "born again" (John 3:3) into the family of God, and then say to the believer, in effect, "You are now complete in Christ, accepted in Him, perfect in your standing before Me in Christ; now *act* like it!" That is God's way.

And to "abide in Christ" is to *appreciate* this fact, and *appropriate* Him every step of the way, yielded to Him, obedient to Him, putting Him first in every department of the life—business, the home, school, companionships, affections, recreations, reading, music, plans—all subject to Him and His priority.

When such is not the case, we must neither expect to "find Him" for personal communion, nor to have His answer to prayer. The Psalmist declares, "If I regard iniquity in my heart, the Lord will not hear me" (Psalm 66:18).

Dr. H. A. Ironside tells of a young woman who, at one time, had made profession of faith in Christ, but who had drifted into the many forms of worldliness so common in our day. She was exceptionally devoted to her father, who was taken ill with a wasting disease. She prayed diligently, over a period of many months, for his recovery, but he grew no better, and finally died. She became very bitter against God, for she felt that He had not dealt fairly and mercifully with her. She went to a pastor friend, and called his attention to the words in John 15:7, ". . . ye shall ask what ye will, and it shall be done unto you."

"You see," she complained, "there is the promise, and God didn't keep His promise. I prayed and prayed, and God didn't answer."

"Oh, but wait a minute," replied the wise pastor. "You

haven't recited the entire promise. The first part of the verse says, 'If ye abide in me, and my words abide in you.' That is the *condition.* Were you abiding in Him when you were in worldly associations on the dance floor? Were you abiding in Him when you were engaging in other questionable amusements? You are attempting to claim a promise to which you are not entitled at all."

The young lady broke down and wept, and said, "Oh, I see it now. I had no right to ask God to restore my father, because I was not abiding in Him."

In verse 7 we find that "the *watchmen* that went about the city" (these we believe to be symbolic of true believers) smote and wounded the Bride while she was away from the Bridegroom, and out of her rightful place of privilege and communion. There were two wrong attitudes in this portion of the episode. First, the Bride was out of her place, and second, the watchmen were supposed to give assistance to those who needed help, and not to *smite* and *wound* those who were lonely and in distress.

What a practical lesson here for us. The Apostle, in Galatians 6:1 and 2, exhorts the saints in tender and yet impelling words, "Brethren, if a man be overtaken in a fault, ye which are spiritual, restore such an one in the spirit of meekness; considering thyself, lest thou also be tempted. Bear ye one another's burdens, and so fulfil the law of Christ." It is no mark of spiritual maturity to *smite* and *wound* the one who is in spiritual distress, whatever the nature of that distress. The exhortation is to "restore," not to criticize; to "bear burdens," not to *bear down* upon them.

The Lord Jesus, as recorded in John 13, washed the feet of the disciples, and in that act gave more than an example of humility. He gave a practical illustration of using the "water of the Word" to cleanse the wayward feet of erring brethren. It will be observed (John 13:5) that after He had washed their feet, He wiped them with the towel. He thoroughly "did the job." Everything He does is perfect and complete. He didn't leave the feet wet and sticky and uncomfortable. He didn't leave them in such a state that others could point them out and say, "Oh, see, he has just had his feet washed." He graciously removed every trace of His gracious work.

There is too much *splashing* of the water of the Word upon erring saints today. When one falls into sin, some true believer, who should know better, is almost certain to take a "bucket-ful of the water of Scripture" and throw it at the offending one and say, "This is what the Bible says about you." And sometimes it is very *hot* water, and sometimes very *cold*. That is not the Lord's way. He doesn't *smite* and *wound,* but mercifully and tenderly and lovingly chastens (child-trains) His own, and then "wipes with the towel."

This art of restoring sinning saints is almost a lost art in the church today. May He, in His infinite tenderness, give us the love and graciousness, as well as the tact and spiritual firmness to be His effective instruments in this important matter.

There is a beautiful Jewish legend regarding bearing one another's burdens. Two brothers had adjoining fields. On the evening after the grain had been cut and shocked, the elder brother said to his wife: "My younger brother is unable to bear the burden and heat of the day. I will arise, take of my shocks, and place them with his, without his knowledge." The younger brother, being actuated by the same benevolent motives, said within himself: "My elder brother has a family, and I have none. I will arise, take of my shocks, and place them with his." Imagine their mutual astonishment when, on the following day, they found their respective shocks the same as they were originally. This went on for several nights, when each resolved in his own mind to stand guard and solve the mystery. They did so, and on the following night they met each other halfway between their respective shocks with their arms full. Tradition says that on that very spot where they met, ground hallowed by such brotherly love and care, the Temple of Solomon was built.

A dear old lady was mourning the loss of her husband, when someone else came to unload all her troubles upon the one who had just lost her lifetime companion. The old lady listened kindly to all the other's difficulty, and when the visitor at last apologized for troubling her at such a time, the old lady answered, "Don't worry about that; I'd always rather carry two pails of water than one." You see, the two pails balance, and so others' difficulties help us to balance our own.

B. 6:3—"I am my beloved's, and my beloved is mine . . ."

For the practical application of this statement, see the remarks concerning verse 16 of Chapter Two.

V. WHAT THE DAUGHTERS OF JERUSALEM SAY ABOUT THE BRIDE

VI. WHAT THE DAUGHTERS OF JERUSALEM SAY ABOUT THE BRIDEGROOM

1. *THE DECLARATION*

A. 5:9—". . . thou fairest among women"
B. 6:1—". . . thou fairest among women"
C. 5:9—"What is thy beloved . . ."
D. 6:1—"Whither (where) is thy beloved . . ."

2. *THE TYPICAL IMPLICATION*

There is that in the true believer which should remind others of Christ. When there is not this likeness to the Lord Jesus, we are not living up to the privileges of our high calling.

These descriptive appellations on the part of the Daughters of Jerusalem (professing believers) indicate that there was a likeness to the Bridegroom in her fairness, as there should be in us, a likeness to our Lord in every phase of our lives and experience. Paul, in II Corinthians 3:17, 18, expresses it in these words, "Now the Lord is that Spirit: and where the Spirit of the Lord is, there is liberty. But we all, with open face beholding as in a glass the glory of the Lord, are changed into the same image from glory to glory, even as by the Spirit of the Lord."

3. *THE NEW TESTAMENT REVELATION*

A. II Corinthians 3:18—"But we all, with open (unveiled) face beholding as in a glass (reflecting as a mirror) the glory of the Lord, are changed (transformed, or transfigured) into the same image from glory to glory, even as by the Spirit of the Lord."

B. II Corinthians 4:6—"For God, who commanded the light to shine out of darkness, hath shined in our hearts, to give the light of the knowledge of the glory of God in the face of Jesus Christ."

C. Matthew 16:13, 15—". . . Whom do men say that I the Son of Man am?" ". . . But whom say ye that I am?"

4. *THE PRACTICAL APPLICATION*

In verse 8 of chapter 5, the Bride had told the Daughters of Jerusalem that she was "sick of (with) love" for her Beloved. Her longing heart, filled to overflowing with such love for him, shone in her countenance, and prompted the Daughters of Jerusalem to address her as "thou fairest among women." What a testimony to the radiance of love!

What do others see when they look at us? Do they see the

reflection in our lives and faces of the "fairest Lord Jesus"? Are they led to confess that the "beauty of the Lord God" is upon us (Psalm 90:17)? The "light of His countenance" is in us and upon us that it—or rather, He—may shine out through us.

It is important to observe here that it is not the Bridegroom who calls the Bride "fairest" in these instances, but others, who are professing believers. The Bridegroom *does* call her "fair" several times (1:8; 1:15; 4:1; 4:7; 4:10), but here her beauty is made a testimony to others. Why? Because she was completely taken up with him.

The real secret of victory, joy, testimony, fruitful service, and liberty in the Christian life is to be truly in love with the Person of the Lord Jesus. This is possible and practical to us who have believed, for "the love of God (and thus the love *for* God) is shed abroad in our hearts by the Holy Ghost" (Rom. 5:5). We love Him with His own love which He, by grace through faith, has bestowed upon us as a free gift.

"Take time to behold Him,
Speak oft with thy Lord;
Abide in Him always,
And feed on His Word.

"Take time to behold Him,
The world rushes on;
Spend much time in secret
With Jesus alone."

Someone has said, "The secret of Christian holiness is heart-occupation with Christ Himself. As we gaze upon Him we become like Him. Do you want to be holy? Spend much time in His presence. Let the loveliness of the risen Lord so fill the vision of your soul that all else is shut out. Then the things of the flesh will shrivel up and disappear, and the things of the Spirit will become supreme in your life. We do not become holy by looking into our own hearts. There we find only corruption. But as we look away from self altogether, 'looking off unto Jesus,' as He is the Object in which we delight, as we contemplate His holiness, purity, love and compassion, His devotion to the Father's will, we shall be transformed, imperceptible to ourselves, perhaps, but none the less surely, into His blessed image. There is no other way whereby we may become practically holy, and be delivered from the power of the flesh and of the principles of the world."

The Daughters of Jerusalem asked two questions of the Bride:

"*What* is thy beloved . . . that thou dost so charge us?"
"*Whither* (where) is thy beloved . . . that we may seek him *with thee?*"

These are the questions which anxious souls are asking of us today:

"*What* is Christ?"
"*Where* is Christ?"

In the proper, scriptural answer to these questions, lies the answer—complete and conclusive— to all *religion, theological error, doubt, cavil, spiritual vagaries,* and *fanatical extremes.*

What is Jesus Christ?

He is God (John 1:1).
He is Creator of all things (Col. 1:16).
He is Sustainer of all things (Col. 1:17).
He is the Revealer of the Father (John 1:18).
He became Man (John 1:14).
He is the complete, all-sufficient Saviour (Acts 4:12).
He is the Risen Christ (I Cor. 15:20).
He is the Living Lord (Acts 2:36).

He is our Representative in heaven (Heb. 9:24).
He is our High Priest (Heb. 4:15).
He is our Advocate (I John 2:1).

Where is Christ?

He is at the right hand of the Father (Heb. 10:12).
He is there in a body of flesh and bone (Luke 24:39).
He is awaiting the signal to come again (Heb. 10:13).
He "liveth in us" (believers) in the Person of God, the Holy Spirit (Gal 2:20; John 14:16-18).

When we who belong to Him are able to answer these questions satisfactorily by word of mouth and, experientially, by life, others will wish to know Him and to follow Him.

Transfixed I stood to witness the death of Christ for me;
The mocking scorn so shameful His suffering on the tree.
How wonderful that Jesus, the Son of God, Most High,
Should stoop in tender pity to suffer and to die.

Transfix my gaze, O Lord, on Thee,
To see more of Thy love to me.

Transformed into Thine image, I would, my Saviour be;
While gazing on Thy beauty, reflecting more of Thee.
Then bless me, Oh, my Saviour, and let my life appear
So pure, and clean, and holy, like glass all crystal clear.

Transform me by Thy wondrous grace,
Imprint Thine image on my face.

Translated! What a prospect for all Thy children here,
Who wait and work with patience, till Thou shalt reappear;
Help me to live still looking, to walk with Thee each day,
That I may answer gladly Thy call to come away.

Translated! Oh, how glad we'll be
To gather Home, dear Lord, with Thee.

—OLIVE V. LUFF

Section Six

SONG OF SOLOMON 6:4-8:14

I. WHAT THE BRIDE SAYS ABOUT THE BRIDEGROOM

1. *THE DECLARATION*

A. 7:10-8:3—"I am my beloved's, and his desire is toward me. Come, my beloved, let us go forth into the field; let us lodge in the villages. Let us get up early to the vineyards; let us see if the vine flourish, whether the tender grape appear, and the pomegranates bud forth . . . His left hand should be under my head, and his right hand should embrace me."

B. 8:14—"Make haste, my beloved, and be thou like to a roe or to a young hart upon the mountains of spices."

2. *THE TYPICAL IMPLICATION*

Surely in the Scriptures under Division "A" we see a clear and challenging reference to personal fellowship with the Lord Jesus as being the incentive to true service.

When the Bride realizes that she is her Beloved's, and the true object of his desire, her next words are, "Come, let us *go forth* into the field . . . let us get up early to the vineyards." There shall be more to say along these lines when we consider the Practical Application of the scene.

In Division "B," the words with which the Song of Songs concludes, there is a perfect typical reference to the last words of the Book of the Revelation, "He which testifieth these things saith, Surely I come quickly. Amen. Even so, come, Lord Jesus."

3. *THE NEW TESTAMENT REVELATION*

A. Acts 1:8—"But ye shall receive power, after that the Holy Ghost is come upon you: and we shall be witnesses unto me both in Jerusalem, and in all Judea, and in Samaria, and unto the uttermost part of the earth."

John 15:16—"Ye have not chosen me, but I have chosen you, and ordained you, that ye should go and bring forth fruit, and that your fruit should remain: that whatsoever ye shall ask of the Father in my name, he may give it you."

B. Revelation 22:17, 20—"And the Spirit and the bride say, Come. And let him that heareth say, Come. And let him that is athirst come. And whosoever will, let him take of the water of life freely. He which testifieth these things saith, Surely I come quickly. Amen. Even so, come, Lord Jesus."

4. *THE PRACTICAL APPLICATION*

A. 7:10-8:3—"I am my beloved's, and his desire is toward me. Come, my beloved, let us go forth into the field; let us lodge in the villages. Let us get up early to the vineyards; let us see if the vine flourish, whether the tender grape appear, and the pomegranates bud forth . . . His left hand should be under my head, and his right hand should embrace me."

When the Bride says, "I am my beloved's, and his desire is toward me," she has struck the sweetest chord of music in the entire Song of Songs. She has finally reached the place where she realizes that the delight of her Beloved is in herself. Self is put out of the picture, she belongs to another, and that other finds all his delight in her.

When the Christian has reached this point in his apprehension and appropriation of divine truth, he has reached the level of spiritual understanding upon which the Lord intends to dwell. The highest level of spiritual life is not expressed in the words, "I am the one who loves the Lord Jesus so much," but rather in the words, "I am the one whom the Lord Jesus loves (John 13:23) and in whom, by His matchless grace, He finds His delight." This is the highest apprehension of Christ, we believe, and the highest appreciation of the grace of God.

The Law cannot produce this happy condition.

Religion cannot give such peace and rest.

The many variations of humanism and behaviorism are powerless to produce this joy.

Only grace, through the Lord Jesus Christ, can do this.

Through grace we who have been born again into the family of God, are able to say, "He knows me; He saw me when I was dead in trespasses and sins; He redeemed me through His precious blood; He clothed me with Himself, the Righteousness of God; He joined me to Himself, so that I am a member of His body; He loves me because of what I am in Him; He delights in me. He knows me perfectly, and loves me with a perfect love."

This perfect apprehension of perfect love is certain to produce a genuine desire for true service. It is only when we fully realize that we are eternally secure in Christ, that we shall be fully prepared to serve Him with liberty of spirit. "*Faith* makes us *walk; Assurance* makes us *run.*"

If we are not convinced of our eternal standing in Christ, but are living in continual uncertainty concerning it, we cannot be set free to serve the Lord, but shall be occupied with ourselves, our fears, our sins, our unworthiness, our doubts, instead of with Him and the eternal need of a world lost in sin.

The phrase "Let us" occurs four times in verses 11 and 12:

"Let us go forth"—that is *service;*
"Let us lodge"—that is *fellowship;*
"Let us get up early"—that is *diligence;*
"Let us see"—that is *spiritual vision.*

In I Corinthians 3:9 the Apostle reminds us that we are "labourers together with God." The words "labourers together" might be translated "workmates." We are workmates of God. There is a difference between "servants" and "workmates." Of course Paul referred to himself as a "bond-servant of Christ," but there is a difference. Pharaoh was a *servant,* even though he had no heart for God, and was against God. Romans 9:17, "For the scripture saith unto Pharaoh, Even for this same purpose have I raised thee up, that I might show my power in thee, and that my name might be declared throughout all the earth."

Nebuchadnezzar was a servant of God, "my servant" (Jer. 25:9), but he was not in personal harmony with God.

God, in His grace, has called us to a higher relationship. If we are to be "workmates," there are several requisites, suggested by J. C. Macaulay in a most helpful message upon this subject:

That we be born again, and thus have a heart for God. There must be compatibility;

That we have an understanding of the plan and purpose of God. We find this in His written Word, the Bible;

That we understand *our* part in God's plan;

That we yield perfect obedience to directions;

That we have love for the brethren;
That we have utter dependence upon the Holy Spirit.

How vital it is that all our "Christian service" be based upon, and flow out from, a realization of our Lord's complete possession of us. He is absolute Sovereign; He has a right to do with us that which He pleases; He is our Power for service; He is our Lord; He is our Strength; He is our Sufficiency. We are not to "work for God"; He will do *His work through us* as we are yielded to Him, spirit, soul, and body.

This truth is expressed beautifully in a poem by Shirley C. Burr, called "Traveling with God."

My plans were made, I thought my path all bright and clear,
My heart with songs o'erflowed, the world seemed full of cheer.
My Lord I wished to serve, to take Him for my Guide,
To keep so close that I could feel Him by my side;
And so I traveled on.

But, suddenly, in skies so clear and full of light,
The clouds fell thick and fast, the days seemed changed to night;
Instead of paths so clear, and full of things so sweet,
Rough things, and thorns, and stones, seemed all about my feet;
I scarce could travel on.

I bowed my head and wondered why this change should come,
And murmured—"Lord, is this because of aught I've done?
Has not the past been full enough of pain and care?
Why should my path again be changed to dark from fair?"
But still I traveled on.

I listened—quiet and still, there came a voice—
"This path is Mine, not thine; I made the choice;
Dear child, *this* service will be the best for thee and Me,
If thou wilt simply trust, and leave the end to Me."
And so *we* travel on.

How vital it is that we learn the secret of true *service, fellowship, diligence,* and *spiritual vision,* as suggested by the fourfold use of the phrase "Let us"; it is occupation with the Lord Jesus Himself.

B. 8:14—"Make haste, my beloved, and be thou like to a roe or to a young hart upon the mountains of spices."

It is beautiful to note that the very last utterance of the Bride is in the form of a plea to the Bridegroom for his intimate presence. She cannot get enough of him!

Is it so with us, fellow believer? *Now* we walk by faith, not by sight (II Cor. 5:7), and although the Holy Spirit dwells within us for the purpose of making Christ real and precious to us personally, yet do we not long for that day when "faith shall be lost in sight," and we shall see Him face to face (I Cor. 13:12).

The Bride could enjoy lovely *thoughts* of the Bridegroom, but she could not be truly satisfied until she could be *with* him. And so with us who belong to Him—we rejoice in the reality of Himself, His love, His grace, His presence—but still, while we are in this world, "we see through a glass darkly" (dimly) (I Cor. 13:12), and eagerly await His coming, when actually we shall *see* Him with these eyes of ours, opened and adapted to eternal glory.

This book may come into the hands of some who have had little, if any, instruction concerning the personal return of the Lord Jesus Christ to this earth. To these may we say that a knowledge of that important truth is absolutely essential to a true understanding of God's purposes in redemption. Christ is coming to this earth again, personally, visibly, bodily, as truly as He came the first time, personally, visibly, and bodily. Consider a few thoughts in connection with this truth:

The fact of His coming again. In the first chapter of the book of Acts, at the ascension of our Lord, after His bodily resurrection, it is recorded that "while they looked stedfastly toward heaven as he went up, behold, two men stood by them in white apparel; which also said, Ye men of Galilee, why stand ye gazing up into heaven? *this same Jesus, which is taken up from you into heaven, shall so come in like manner as ye have seen him go into heaven.*" This is such a clear, definite statement that it permits of no "interpretation." It must be believed or disbelieved. It cannot be "interpreted." As He left this earth personally, visibly, bodily —not in a mere "spiritual" sense—so He will come again.

The manner of His coming again. There are to be two main aspects, or phases, of His return. First, He will come *for* His own people. This is declared in two principal Scripture portions, John 14:1-3, and I Thessalonians 4:13-18. In both of these texts we are informed that the Lord Jesus is coming again to receive all His true believers, those who have died, and those who are alive and remain unto His coming. He shall descend from heaven into the air, and we shall be changed "in the twinkling of an eye" (I Cor. 15:52) and be caught up to meet Him. The second phase of His coming might be described, in a general way, as His coming *with* His own people to rule and reign over the earth (I Thess. 3:13). We who have been saved by grace through faith in the precious blood of Christ—after we have been caught up to meet Him in the air—shall return with Him to share the glory of His reign over the earth (II Tim. 2:12; Rev. 5:10).

The importance of His coming again. In a very real sense, the completion of our salvation awaits the second coming of Christ (Heb. 9:28). In Romans 8:23 we learn that "we ourselves groan within ourselves, waiting for the adoption, to wit, the redemption of our body." Salvation extends to spirit, soul, and body—the three parts of man—and when our Lord comes again, our bodies shall be redeemed, and changed, into the likeness of His body of glory (Phil. 3:20, 21).

Rewards for the believer at His coming again. Salvation is a free gift, not a reward in any sense. But rewards are given to Christians for faithfulness in service. These will be given at the judgment seat of Christ when He comes again (I Cor. 3:11-15).

The results of His coming again. Israel as a nation will be regathered and restored to a place of blessing (Rom. 11:26; also see scores of references in the Old Testament Prophetic Books). There will be a Millennium of righteousness and peace (Rev. 20:1-6). There will be new heavens and a new earth (II Pet. 3:13; Acts 3:21). The nations will be judged (Matt. 25:31-46). Satan and the wicked shall be cast into the lake of fire (Rev. 20:10-15).

The practical effect of His coming again. To the enlightened believer, the moment by moment looking for the Lord to return is a "blessed hope" (Titus 2:13), and has a most salutary effect upon his Christian life and service. As we live, day by day, with the prospect that "He may come today," we find our words and deeds solemnized and purified. And the more eagerly we are looking for Him, the more eagerly and diligently are we seeking to bring others to a saving knowledge of Him.

"Caught up! Caught up! no wing required,
Caught up to Him by love inspired,
To meet Him in the air;
Spurning the earth with upward bound,
Nor casting a single glance around,
Nor listing a single earth-born sound,
Caught up in the radiant air.

"Caught up with rapture and surprise,
Caught up, our fond affections rise
Our coming Lord to meet;
Hearing the trumpet's glorious sound,

Soaring to join the rising crowd,
Gazing beyond the parted cloud
Beneath His piercéd feet!

"O blesséd, O thrice-blesséd word!
To be forever with the Lord,
In heavenly beauty fair!
Up, Up! We long to hear the cry;
Up, Up! our absent Lord draws nigh;
Yes, in the twinkling of an eye,
Caught up in the radiant air!"

II. WHAT THE BRIDEGROOM SAYS ABOUT THE BRIDE

1. *THE DECLARATION*

A. 6:4—"Thou art beautiful, O my love, as Tirzah, comely as Jerusalem, terrible as an army with banners."

B. 6:5-7; 7:1-6—"Turn away thine *eyes* from me, for they have overcome me: thy *hair* is as a flock of goats that appear from Gilead. Thy *teeth* are as a flock of sheep which go up from the washing, whereof every one beareth twins, and there is not one barren among them. As a piece of a pomegranate are thy *temples* within thy locks . . .

How beautiful are thy *feet with shoes,* O prince's daughter! The joints of thy *thighs* are like jewels, the work of the hands of a cunning workman.

Thy *navel* is like a round goblet, which wanteth not liquor: thy *belly* is like an heap of wheat set about with lilies. Thy *two breasts* are like two young roes that are twins. Thy *neck* is as a tower of ivory; thine *eyes* like the fishpools in Heshbon, by the gate of Bath-rabbim: thy *nose* is as the tower of Lebanon which looketh toward Damascus. Thine *head* upon thee is like Carmel, and the *hair* of thine head like purple; the king is held in the galleries.

How fair and how pleasant art *thou,* O love, for delights!"

C. 6:9—"My dove, my undefiled, is but *one;* she is the only *one* of her mother, she is the choice *one* of her that bare her."

D. 7:7-9—"This thy stature is like to a palm tree, and thy breasts to clusters of grapes. I said, I will go up to the palm tree, I will take hold of the boughs thereof: now also thy breasts shall be as clusters of the vine, and the smell of thy nose like apples; And the roof of thy mouth like the best wine for my beloved, that goeth down sweetly, causing the lips of those that are asleep to speak."

E. 8:13—"Thou that dwellest in the gardens, the companions hearken to thy voice: cause me to hear it."

2. *THE TYPICAL IMPLICATION*

These portions suggest several typical implications, and while we shall discuss them in detail under "Practical Application," we mention them here:

A. 6:4—We find here, in the words "beautiful," "comely," and "terrible," the threefold suggestion of *position* in Christ, *testimony* before others, and *victory* in Christian experience.

B. 6:5-7; 7:1-6—Very similar expressions to these were used by the Bridegroom in describing the Bride in Chapter Four. But since that time, the Bride has broken fellowship and communion with her beloved, and has returned to him. Thus we see a type of the backslider who confesses and forsakes his backslidings and returns to the Lord, to receive assurance of his perfect standing and relationship in grace.

C. 6:9—A beautiful suggestion that while the Lord loves and cares for *all* His own, He loves and cares for *each*. Also a declaration of our oneness with Him and all the family of God.

D. 7:7-9—The palm tree furnishes a lovely type of the believer in many respects. We shall examine this symbol in detail in a later paragraph.

E. 8:13—In this verse we see a typical reference to the believer as a gospel witness; to the assurance that when the gospel is proclaimed there will be fruit; and to the joy which comes to the heart of our Lord when the multitudes of the redeemed join in anthems of praise, of joy, of thanksgiving, of worship, unto Him.

3. *THE NEW TESTAMENT REVELATION*

A. John 15:9—"As the Father hath loved me, so have I loved you: continue ye in my love."
Acts 1:8—". . . ye shall be witnesses unto me."
Romans 8:37—". . . in all these things we are more than conquerors through him that loved us."

B. I John 1:9—"If we confess our sins, he is faithful and just to forgive us our sins, and to cleanse us from all unrighteousness."

I Corinthians 11:31-32—"For if we would judge ourselves, we should not be judged. But when we are judged, we are chastened of the Lord, that we should not be condemned with the world."

C. Galations 3:28—"There is neither Jew nor Greek (Gentile), there is neither bond nor free, there is neither male nor female: for ye are all one in Christ Jesus."

John 17:21—"That they all may be one; as thou, Father, art in me, and I in thee, that they also may be one in us: that the world may believe that thou hast sent me."

D. II Peter 3:18—"But grow in grace, and in the knowledge of our Lord and Saviour Jesus Christ." I Peter 2:2—"As newborn babes, desire the sincere milk of the word, that ye may grow thereby." Ephesians 4:15—". . . grow up into (unto) him (Christ) in all things."

E. Hebrews 4:12—"For the word of God is quick (living), and powerful (operative), and sharper than any two-edged sword, piercing even to the dividing asunder of soul and spirit, and of the joints and marrow, and is a discerner (critic) of the thoughts and intents of the heart."

Luke 15:7—"I say unto you, that likewise joy shall be in heaven over one sinner that repenteth . . ."

4. *THE PRACTICAL APPLICATION*

A. 6:4—"Thou art beautiful, O my love, as Tirzah, comely as Jerusalem, terrible as an army with banners."

There is a lovely order in the use of these adjectives, "beautiful," "comely," and "terrible" as applied by the Bridegroom to his Bride. "Tirzah" means "she will delight," and "Jerusalem" means "teach ye peace."

We see the threefold suggestion of our *position* in Christ, our privilege to *witness* for Him, and the assurance of our *victory* in Him. Yea, He *is* our Victory.

"Thou art beautiful . . . as Tirzah." Again we are reminded that we, clothed with the Lord Jesus Christ, the Righteousness of God, are precious and beautiful to our Lord. We are "complete in Him" (Col. 2:10). We are complete and accepted, not in ourselves, not in our sincerity, not in our ecclesiastical affiliations, not in church ordinances, not in our good deeds or good intentions, but *in Him*. So he may look upon us, clothed with Himself, and delight in us. Unspeakable grace!

"Comely as Jerusalem." Not only has He redeemed us to enjoy this communion and fellowship with Himself, but to be witnesses in a world of darkness and sin. He said, as recorded in Acts 1:8, ". . . ye *shall be* witnesses." This is not so much a command as it is a prophecy. It is His purpose that each born-again believer be a witness for Him. The *kind* of witnesses we are depends upon our yieldedness to and dependence upon Him. "Jerusalem" means "teach ye peace," and that is our mission, to proclaim the glorious fact that "He is our peace" (Eph. 2:14), and that "He hath made peace by the blood of His cross" (Col. 1:20). Peace with God has been made (Rom. 5:1). The gift of eternal life (Rom. 6:23) is absolutely free to whomsoever will receive it (John 3:16). May it please Him to make us "comely" witnesses. God, the Holy Spirit, dwells within us, and will use us to shine for Him, just where we are, as we trust wholly His person and power.

"Terrible as an army with banners." This military figure sounds a bit strange in this setting, but it has a most important connotation. It suggests victory to the child of God. It is a way of saying to us, "You are complete in Christ; He is all that you need for witnessing and service; and He *is* the armour of God (Eph. 6:10-18) by which you 'stand against the wiles of the devil.' " The apostle declares in II Corinthians 2:14, "Now thanks be unto God, which always causes us to triumph (leadeth us in triumph) in Christ, and maketh manifest the savour of his knowledge by us in every place." "We are more than conquerors through him that loved us" (Rom. 8:37).

It is encouraging to note the sequence of the thought in this verse:

"beautiful"—*acceptance* and *position*
"comely"—*witness* and *service*
"terrible"—*victory* and *overcoming*

The fruitful service, and the life of victory to the Christian is based upon, and flows out from, his absolutely indissoluble union with Christ, and his eternally unchangeable position in Christ. Make no mistake about it. That is God's way. There is no other way in His plan. We may substitute our own theories of holiness, of growth, of service, and victory, but only God's ways are acceptable to Him.

B. 6:5-7; 7:1-6—". . . How fair and how pleasant art *thou,* O love, for delights!"

It is interesting here to observe that again the Bridegroom goes into detailed ecstasy in enumerating the various features of the Bride in which he finds delight. Two things especially claim our attention. First, the fact that his expressions of affection are made *after* a period of broken communion, or, as we might say, "backsliding." When we consider this subject, we must realize two things, namely, that the word "backsliding" is not found in the New Testament, and also that there is a vast difference between "backsliding" and "apostasy." A *believer* may *backslide,* but only an *unbeliever* may *apostatize.* Backsliding is, as the word implies, sliding backward in one's Christian life; but it does not alter true relationship to God through the Lord Jesus

Christ. On the other hand, apostasy is the departure from a *professed* position or religious allegiance. Those who apostatize have never been born again at all, but have given fealty to a creed, or have professed loyalty to a cause, or even to the person of Christ Himself. But, having no life relationship to Him through the new birth, apostasy is possible to these. Peter is the outstanding biblical example of *backsliding;* Judas of *apostasy. Backsliding* is possible of cure; *apostasy* is incurable. When one is out of fellowship with Christ through backsliding, two courses are open to him; he may recognize his sin and backslidden state, confess it and return to communion and blessing (I John 1:9); or he may procrastinate, and await the chastening of the Lord and be *brought* back through sorrow or affliction. Our Lord is faithful, and will not allow His own to remain away from Himself indefinitely. In I Corinthians 11:31, 32, we have the clear statement of the divine procedure in this matter: "For if we would judge ourselves, we should not be judged. But when we are judged, we are chastened of the Lord, *that we should not be condemned with the world.*" That is the remedial aspect of chastening. It is one of the instruments of *grace,* employed by the Lord to guarantee that the true believer shall not be condemned (Rom. 8:1). How complete is our Lord's provision for us!

Someone has said that the various attitudes of Christians toward chastening may be described by the actions of three birds in the rain. The *duck* in the rain apparently is not conscious of the water upon its back, but indifferently sheds it. Some Christians seem to have a stoical indifference to the chastening hand of the Lord, and their lives seem not to be benefited by it. The *hen* in the rainstorm rebels against it, and seeks to avoid it as much as possible. Some believers rebel against the heavenly Father's chastening hand, and employ every conceivable means of avoiding or eliminating it. But the *robin* sings its sweetest song in the rain. Some of the children of God have seen the hand and purpose of God's loving heart in the chastening, and have sung the sweet songs of trust, of joy, and of praise, through the training experience.

Let not the backslider despair, but come back with confession, and confidence, that the Lord will use him mightily, as Peter, when he turned again, was used to strengthen the brethren (Luke 22:32). The annals of Christian experience are filled with the cases of those who have returned unto the Lord from "wandering in the far country," and have been "vessels meet for the Master's use." Just this further word: While it is the privilege of the backslider not to *despair,* let not the believer *presume* upon God's mercy and forgiving grace! Complete provision has been made in Christ, so that we, in complete dependence upon Him, need not wander *into* the "far country." It is blessed to know that we may be restored when we fall into sin, but it is more blessed to know that we need not wander from Him!

The second thing to claim our attention in this section is the expression in the first verse of Chapter Seven, "How beautiful are thy feet *with shoes."* This is the one instance where an article of wearing apparel is associated, in the description, with the mention of the physical features. We think of two Scripture portions here: Isaiah 52:7, "How beautiful upon the mountains are the feet of him that bringeth good tidings, that publisheth peace; that bringeth good tidings of good, that publisheth salvation"; and Ephesians 6:15, "having . . . your feet shod with the preparation of the gospel of peace." Not only does our Lord *give* peace, but He *is* our peace—peace to the repentant sinner, peace to the anxious believer, and peace to the one who goes forth to tell others of the Saviour.

C. 6:9—"My dove, my undefiled, is but *one;* she is the only *one* of her mother, she is the choice *one* of her that bare her."

How beautifully this reminds the individual child of God that he is just as precious to his Lord, just as truly the object of His care, as if he were the only one in the entire universe who belonged to Christ! "One"—how wonderful! Are you fearful, child of God? Are you discouraged? Tested? Heartsick and weary? Lift up your head and rejoice. You are dear to Him. You are *one* with Him, and, as our verse suggests, "one" *to* Him.

D. 7:7-9—"this thy stature is like to a palm tree."

In "Joined to the Lord," by Annie W. Marston, there is an instructive reference to the simile employed here. "The 'stature' of the palm tree is always *straight* and *upright,* never stooping or bending this way or that; unmoved by any passing breeze; stretching ever upward with a steady, unswerving aim, refusing to be pressed or bent downwards, no matter what heavy weights may be attached to it; reminding us of the steady singleness of aim spoken of by the apostle who said, 'This one thing I do; forgetting the things which are behind, and stretching forward to the things which are before, I press on toward the goal unto the prize of the high calling of God in Christ Jesus' (Phil. 3:13, 14, R.V.). The palm tree gives food, and rest, and shelter: and we have been 'ordained' that we should bring forth fruit (John 15:16), and it is our privilege to give shelter and rest and refreshment to the weary and distressed.

"The palm tree grows in the most unlikely places, in sandy deserts where nothing else can grow. It thrives in the midst of barrenness, and dearth, and drought, because it strikes its roots ever deeper and deeper into the dry soil, and draws moisture and nourishment from hidden springs deep down beyond the sight of man: therefore its life and growth are maintained where there is apparently nothing for it to feed upon: and therefore men who would otherwise perish for lack of food and drink, are kept alive and nourished by it.

"How well we can understand what follows. 'I said, I will *go up* to the palm tree, I will take hold of the boughs thereof.' It looks so beautiful in the distance; so noble, so fruitful, so thriving. I will go close up to it, and take hold of it, and examine it near at hand, and see whether upon close inspection it is just the same as it appears when seen from a distance. Such a natural thing to do. How often the same thought has crossed our mind. So-and-so seems to be such a lovely Christian; so strong and straight and fruitful; how I should like to know him well. I wonder is he just as holy and helpful in intimate friendship as on distant acquaintance? Do we not all know something of the disappointment of finding, when the opportunity has been given to us of going up to the palm tree and 'taking hold of the boughs thereof,' that it was not at all the same when seen near as when seen from afar, and we have wished that we had never known anything nearer than the slight acquaintance which was so much the better? And, on the other hand, what a joy and gladness it has been when, after getting very near and seeing in everyday life those whose distant appearance had so attracted us, we have found that they were *just the same* near at hand as they seemed afar off, just as Christlike, and just as fruitful: *they bore close inspection.* Is it so with us? Or does intimate friendship with us end in disappointment to those who come near enough to us to find out what we really are?"

E. 8:13—"Thou that dwellest in the gardens, the companions hearken to thy voice: cause me to hear it."

Here we are invited by the Lord to praise Him—". . . thy voice: cause me to hear it." "Whoso offereth praise glorifieth me" (Psalm 50:23). He rejoices to hear His people proclaiming the message of the gospel throughout the whole earth, so that all may hear. But, also, He rejoices to hear "the voice" of the believer in words of praise, prayer, thanksgiving and worship, addressed to Himself.

There is a difference between *thanksgiving* and *praise. Thanksgiving* is the expression on the part of the believer toward God because of what God *does* and *gives. Praise* is the believer's expression toward God because of what God *is*. Our Father loves to have us tell Him that He *is* to us all that He claims to be, and all that we need, or desire. In such a day of confusion and rush, how truly do we need to pause and let our blessed Lord "hear our voice." Not merely in petition, but in worship and praise.

III. WHAT THE BRIDE SAYS ABOUT HERSELF

1. *THE DECLARATION*

A. 7:12, 13—". . . there will I give thee my loves. The mandrakes give a smell, and at our gates are all manner of pleasant fruits, new and old, which I have laid up for thee, O my beloved."

B. 8:10—"I am a wall, and my breasts like towers: then was I in his eyes as one that found favour."

C. 8:12—"My vineyard, which is mine, is before me: thou, O Solomon, must have a thousand, and those that keep the fruit thereof two hundred."

2. *THE TYPICAL IMPLICATION*

In these words of the Bride, we have the final expressions of personal yieldedness and affection. This scene is typical of the Christian who has come to see that all that he is, (7:12, 13), all the service he can render (8:10), and all his possessions (8:12), are only possible because he belongs wholly to Christ.

3. *THE NEW TESTAMENT REVELATION*

A. Philippians 3:7-10—"But what things were gain to me, those I counted loss for Christ. Yea doubtless, and I count all things but loss for the excellency of the knowledge of Christ Jesus my Lord: for whom I have suffered the loss of all things, and do count them but dung, that I may win Christ, And be found in him, not having mine own righteousness, which is of the law, but that which is through the faith of Christ, the righteousness which is of God by faith: That I may know him, and the power of his resurrection, and the fellowship of his sufferings, being made conformable unto his death."

B. James 2:14-17—"What doth it profit, my brethren, though a man say he hath faith, and have not works? can (that kind of) faith save him? If a brother or sister be naked, and destitute of daily food, And one of you say unto them, Depart in peace, be ye warmed and filled; notwithstanding ye give them not those things which are needful to the body; what doth it profit? Even so faith, if it hath not works, is dead, being alone."

C. I Corinthians 3:23—". . . ye are Christ's; and Christ is God's."

I Corinthians 6:19, 20—"What? know ye not that your body is the temple of the Holy Ghost which is in you, which ye have of (from) God, and ye are not your own?

For ye are (were) bought with a price: therefore glorify God in your body . . ."

4. *THE PRACTICAL APPLICATION*

In these statements by the Bride, we see the three main factors which are characteristic of the Christian who is enjoying unbroken communion and fellowship with his Lord: first, the sweet savour and fragrance of genuine worship (7:12, 13); second, the strength and suppleness of helpful service toward others; and third, the complete yieldedness of one's possessions as well as oneself, realizing that all that we have, as well as all that we *are,* belongs unto the Lord Jesus.

When we are enjoying the right relationship to Christ, we shall enjoy the proper relationship with others, and there will be no question concerning the matter of stewardship of money, time, and other material possessions. The fact is that not merely one-tenth, or one-fifth, or one-half of all we possess belongs to the Lord, but rather that *all* is His, and we are but stewards of His possessions. When we fully realize this, how vitally it changes our attitude toward the use of our money and other property. We cannot make Him rich by giving unto Him, nor can we impoverish Him by withholding our gifts. But *our souls* are made rich or poor by the use we make of His property which He has entrusted to us.

IV. WHAT THE BRIDEGROOM SAYS ABOUT HIMSELF

1. *THE DECLARATION*

A. 6:11, 12—"I went down into the garden of nuts (spices) to see the fruits of the valley, and to see whether the vine flourished, and the pomegranates budded. Or ever I was aware, my soul made me like the chariots of Ammi-nadib."

2. *THE TYPICAL IMPLICATION*

Surely we see here clearly the typical suggestion of our blessed Lord, who left the glory He had with the Father before the world was (John 17:5), and came to this world of sin and woe, to give Himself a ransom for sinners, that He might finish the work of redemption, and bring multitudes of redeemed humanity to eternal fellowship with Himself (Phil. 2:5-11).

The marginal translation of verse 12 renders it, "Or ever I was aware, my soul set me on the chariots of my willing people." This has a twofold implication; first, it indicates that, as a result of the voluntary humbling of the Lord Jesus, in taking upon Himself the "likeness of men" (Phil. 2:7), and the eternal value of His death and resurrection, as well as His work as High Priest and Advocate, He has a Body of "willing people," the saints of all dispensations who have, by faith, received Him as Saviour, and have been born again into the family of God. Second, we are reminded that in a day which we believe to be not far distant, His earthly people, Israel, now scattered throughout the nations of the earth, and judicially blinded now because of their rejection of Christ as Messiah, shall be regathered and made "willing in the day of His power" (Psa. 110:3). What a glorious day awaits the fulfillment of God's purposes for the Jewish people!

3. *THE NEW TESTAMENT REVELATION*

A. Philippians 2:5-11—"Let this mind be in you, which was also in Christ Jesus: Who, being in the form (rank) of God, thought it not robbery (a thing to be grasped after) to be equal with God: But made himself of no reputation, and took upon him the form (rank) of a servant, and was made in the likeness of men: And being found in

> fashion as a man, he humbled himself, and became obedient unto death, even the death of the cross. Wherefore God also hath highly exalted him, and given him a name which is above every name: That at the name of Jesus every knee should bow, of things in heaven, and things in earth, and things under the earth; And that every tongue should confess that Jesus Christ is Lord, to the glory of God the Father."
>
> I Peter 5:5—". . . all of you be subject one to another, and be clothed with humility."

4. *THE PRACTICAL APPLICATION*

In the phrase "I went down" we find the secret of all true exaltation. The way *up* is *down*. As a great Bible teacher of another generation puts it, "The only ennobling attitude of man is that of subjection."

The Lord Jesus, in His willing humiliation, has given us the example of this eternal principle. And He has said, "For whosoever exalteth himself shall be abased, and he that humbleth himself shall be exalted" (Luke 14:11). And also, ". . . If any man will come after me, *let him deny himself,* and take up his cross daily, and follow me" (Luke 9:23).

The sinner cannot be saved until he is ready to "go down" to the place where he is willing to acknowledge that he has nothing of his own righteousness or merit acceptable to God, and that he must receive eternal life as a free gift of God's grace, wholly apart from any consideration of human merit or desert. Zacchaeus climbed a tree to see the Lord Jesus (Luke 19:1-10). But he was ordered to "come down," and was told that salvation *had come to him*. Multitudes today are climbing trees of "religion," of "good works," of "sincerity," of "religious ordinances," of "memberships" of various kinds, hoping thus to reach the Saviour. But His word is still "come down, I am Salvation, and I have come to you." "He that believeth on Me hath everlasting life."

The *believer* who would be fruitful in the service of the Lord must "go down" to the place of acknowledgment that "without me ye can do nothing," as the Lord Jesus said (John 15:5). There must be no energy of the flesh in our service. There must be no false idea of pride in our service. We are permitted to serve by the grace of God. Fruit that is produced as the result of our service, is produced by the Holy Spirit working through us.

What a difference it would make in every phase of our lives as Christians if this truth were consistently and conscientiously applied. If we are willing to be subject, instead of insisting upon the preeminence, how our Lord should be glorified in and through us! In social contacts, business connections, family lives, and church activities, how this spirit of the Lord Jesus is needed! May He, by His grace, grant it unto us.

F. B. Meyer once said, "I used to think that God's gifts were on shelves one *above* the other, and that the *taller* we grew in Christian character, the easier we could reach them. I now find that God's gifts are on shelves one beneath the other; and that it is not a question of growing taller, but of stooping *lower,* and that we have to go *down,* always *down* to get His best gifts."

V. WHAT THE DAUGHTERS OF JERUSALEM SAY ABOUT THE BRIDE

1. *THE DECLARATION*

A. 6:10—"Who is she that looketh forth as the morning, fair as the moon, clear as the sun, and terrible as an army with banners?"

B. 6:13—"Return, return, O Shulamite; return, return, that we may look upon thee. What will ye see in the Shulamite? As it were the company of two armies."

C. 8:5—"Who is this that cometh up from the wilderness, leaning upon her beloved?"

2. *THE TYPICAL IMPLICATION*

In these questions and exhortation on the part of the Daughters of Jerusalem (professing believers, some of whom may be true believers—together composing that which we call "Christendom"), we have a typical presentation of the genuine attractiveness of the yielded Christian. There is a double reference, as we shall see in a later paragraph, to the transformation which is clearly apparent in the believer who is enjoying true communion with his Lord; and to the glory which is yet in prospect for all believers, when our Lord shall come again to receive us, and when we shall be changed into the likeness of His glory (I Thess. 4:13-18; Phil. 3:20, 21).

3. *THE NEW TESTAMENT REVELATION*

A. I Thessalonians 1:9, 10—". . . how ye turned to

B. God from idols to serve the living and true God; And to *wait for his Son from heaven . . .*"

Titus 2:13—". . . Looking for that blessed hope, and the glorious appearing of the great God and our Saviour Jesus Christ."

Hebrews 12:2—"Looking unto Jesus . . ."

II Corinthians 3:18—"But we all, with open (unveiled) face beholding as in a glass (reflecting as a mirror) the glory of the Lord, are changed into the same image from glory to glory, even as by the Spirit of the Lord."

Revelation 3:4—". . . they shall walk with me in white . . ."

Colossians 3:4—"When Christ, who is our life, shall appear, then shall ye also appear with him in glory."

John 16:33—". . . be of good cheer; I have overcome the world."

I John 5:4—"For whatsoever is born of God overcometh the world: and this is the victory that overcometh the world, even our faith."

C. I Corinthians 15:58—"Therefore, my beloved brethren, be ye steadfast, unmoveable, always abounding in the work of the Lord, forasmuch as ye know that your labour is not in vain in the Lord."

4. *THE PRACTICAL APPLICATION*

A. 6:10—"Who is she that looketh forth as the morning, fair as the moon, clear as the sun, and terrible as an army with banners?"

B. 6:13—"Return, return, O Shulamite; return, return, that we may look upon thee. What will ye see in the Shulamite? As it were the company of two armies."

In verse 10 there are four things said of the Bride:

a. she looketh forth as the morning;
b. she is fair as the moon;
c. she is clear as the sun;
d. she is terrible as an army with banners.

There is practical and inspiring truth here for the Christian.

a. ". . . looketh forth as the morning." It is important to note that this is no indifferent or careless looking referred to here, but a "looking *forth,*" eager, sincere, expectant. It reminds us of the kind of looking for the Lord to return mentioned in I Thessalonians 1:10, "... to wait for his Son from heaven." This is no idle, lazy waiting, but rather a "standing on tip-toe" kind of waiting, which occupies its time with Holy Spirit directed service. The believer who is really "looking forth" in this sense, is not sitting idly, with folded hands, waiting for his Lord, but is looking *forth* upon the fields (John 4:35), and sees them "white already to harvest." He looks forth "as the morning," with all the freshness, beauty, and anticipation of joyous service; not burdened, anxious, tense and nervous activity, but as one who has taken upon him the Lord's yoke which is easy and light (Matt. 11:28-30). He knows that there will be reward and unspeakable joy when his Lord comes again. And so he "looketh forth as the morning."

b. "... fair as the moon." There are several words in the original language of the Old Testament which are translated "moon," but this one is from a word whose root meaning is "to be white." Thus it suggests the moon, not in eclipse, or in partial view, but the *full moon,* with its face toward the sun, reflecting the full radiance of that brilliant orb. There is no "earth" between the sun and the moon in this scene before us, to cause eclipse and darkness, but reflecting as a mirror the glory of the Lord (II Cor. 3:18). What a privilege is ours—to be mirrors for Jesus Christ. "White" in Scripture is associated with overcoming, as well as practical righteousness. This is gloriously possible to us as we receive the full radiance of the personal glory of Christ, with "nothing between."

c. ". . . clear as the sun." This speaks of what we are now, *positionally* in Christ, and what we shall be when He appears, and we shall be with Him, and transformed into His lovely likeness. We shall have glorified bodies, like unto His body of glory (Phil. 3:21). No more weakness, sickness, pain, weariness, or death.

d. ". . . terrible as an army with banners." We saw, when considering the Bridegroom's statement in verse 4 of this same chapter, that this expression signifies victory and overcoming in the Christian life. Here the Daughters of Jerusalem apply the same form of expression to the Bride which is used by the Bridegroom. This furnishes to us the further practical truth that victory in Christian experience has not merely the *Godward* aspect, but *manward* as well. When, by faith, we overcome "the world, the flesh, and the devil," others will take note of it, and some thus will be led to the Lord.

We are reminded of Paul and Silas in the Philippian jail. In the midst of circumstances which were unjustly imposed upon them, and in which they were humanly helpless to find a remedy, we learn that "at midnight Paul and Silas prayed, and sang praises unto God" (Acts 16:25). That was a real evidence of victory, and God must have rejoiced to hear those sweet songs at the "midnight hour" of their experience. But that was not all. The same verse (v.25) further records, "and the prisoners heard them." What a blessed report! When we fully trust the Lord, even when we cannot fully *trace* Him, some "Daughters of Jerusalem" will take note of the victory displayed in us, and will be encouraged and blessed.

C. 8:5—"Who is this that cometh up from the wilderness, leaning upon her beloved?"
So many practical truths flood the mind and heart as we attempt to apply this thought to the relationship between the believer and the Lord Jesus.

a. We were "in the wilderness." We "were dead in trespasses and sins" (Eph. 2:1). We were in the "horrible pit . . . and miry clay" (Psalm 40:2). We were under condemnation with the world. We were lost, and wandering in the wilderness (Luke 15:4). But, thank God, Christ "came to seek and to save that which was lost" (Luke 19:10). He found us, and brought us "on his shoulders, rejoicing" (Luke 15:5).

b. ". . . cometh up." There should be continual progress in the Christian life. You ask a small boy how old he is, and very likely he will say, "I'm ten, *going on* eleven," or "eleven, *going on* twelve." They are always "going on." That is the way it should be with us. We should "grow *in* grace and knowledge of our Lord and Saviour Jesus Christ" (II Pet. 3:18). We do not grow *into* grace, but, having been brought *into* grace by God's power, through the finished work of Chirst, we grow *in* grace. We grow as we eat the proper food—the Word of God; as we have proper drink—the Person of Christ (John 7:37-39); as we breathe proper air—the atmosphere of Holy Spirit directed prayer; and as we have proper exercise—testimony and service.

Go on going on, Christian,
Go on going on;
Though the day be dark and dreary
There is light ahead, and surely
Waiting won't be long;
Go on going on, Christian,
Go on going on;
Christ the Saviour's just the same
Yesterday, today, forever,
Go on going on!

c. ". . . leaning on her beloved." She has reached the place of complete confidence and trust. She has found *all* her satisfaction in the Beloved. She has found that His "strength is made perfect in weakness" (II Cor. 12:9) and so she leans upon Him. No more does she desire to wander in the wilderness of sin, of broken communion, of interrupted fellowship, but now she finds Him to be her All in All.

CHRIST—absolutely necessary;
CHRIST—instantly accessible;
CHRIST—exclusively sufficient;
CHRIST—perennially satisfying.